Law Firm KM: Driving Practice Innovation and Redefining Service Delivery

Edited by LAURA SLATER

Head of legal publishing
Fiona Fleming

Publisher
Helen Donegan

Managing editor
Emma Reitano

Editor
Laura Slater

Published by ARK Group:

UK, Europe and Asia office
6–14 Underwood Street
London, N1 7JQ
United Kingdom
Tel: +44(0) 207 566 5792
publishing@ark-group.com

North America office
4408 N. Rockwood Drive, Suite 150
Peoria IL 61614
United States
Tel: +1 (309) 495 2853
publishingna@ark-group.com

www.ark-group.com

Layout by Paul Barrett Book Production, Cambridge

Printed in the United Kingdom by Ashford Colour Press Limited, Gosport, Hampshire

ISBN: 978-1-78358-229-7

A catalogue record for this book is available from the British Library

ARK Group is a division of Wilmington plc.
The company is registered in England & Wales with company number 2931372 GB.
Registered office: 6–14 Underwood Street, London N1 7JQ. VAT Number: GB 899 3725 51.

Contents

Part Two: Case studies

Executive summary

We are all aware of what constitutes the "new normal" in the legal profession: "cost-conscious" clients with an eye on service delivery and far greater leverage than ever before; expectations of greater transparency and higher quality standards; and increased competition from both within and outside the legal market, and from all the resources the internet has to offer. For many law firms, the new normal has meant lower demand coupled with increased competition, making the need to consider new service models, pricing structures, and innovation essential to survival.

Knowledge management is evolving in line with the demands that are reshaping the business of law and redefining service delivery models. Increasingly, law firms are seeing its potential as an "organizational capability" for leveraging the firm's experience, data, and intellectual capital as a strategic resource. In *Law Firm KM: Driving Practice Innovation and Redefining Service Delivery* some of the best minds in the legal and business consulting industries bring their knowledge and experience to bear on the key challenges and opportunities of using KM as a strategic tool.

This book is divided into two parts. Part One shines a light on how knowledge management professionals can support law firm and in-house needs, and considers some of the challenges faced by KM professionals (including the difficulty of persuading fee earners to spare billable time to embed their knowledge into the firm's systems, and proving ROI on KM initiatives). The second part of this book comprises practical guidance in the form of case studies from UK and US law firms that are leading the way in integrating knowledge management principles into their overall firm strategy.

Part One opens with a chapter from Keith Lipman from Prosperoware and Toby Brown from Akin Gump who demonstrate how aligning knowledge management with law firm strategy can help a firm to increase operational efficiency at every level of the business. It outlines how, in doing so, a firm can significantly improve its ability to meet client expectations on pricing and predictability, and help to ensure profitably in a cost-conscious market – a true win-win.

As the author of the book's second chapter notes, "pricing without knowledge management is just guessing". And, in a climate where clients are increasingly subjecting firms' bills to scrutiny, demanding discounts, or putting the squeeze on hourly rates, guess-work is simply not good enough. Accurate and transparent pricing not only gives clients a favorable impression of your experience, it also helps firms to meet client budgetary requirements while ensuring matter profitability. Chapter 2 by Matt Laws covers methods for and the benefits of incorporating KM into the pricing of legal engagements.

Chapter 3 moves on to the sometimes difficult topic of measuring the success of law firm KM. What is the value of knowledge management to a law firm? How can it be measured? How can it be used to differentiate one firm from another? Mark Gould answers these essential questions that should form the foundation of any law firm's KM initiatives if they are to be judged as a long-term success.

Chapter 4 comes from Harriet Creamer who looks at how clients benefit when firms align KM with their business development processes. She highlights the benefits of a KM team's engagement in client relationships, and provides examples of how firms can take – and are taking – this beyond business development, instead focusing on finding new and innovative ways of working with clients and meeting their expectations in terms of speed, cost, and quality.

Much legal work still relies on written work product; it follows that the firms that produce a high quality product adding value for clients and saving the firm time and money will be more successful than those that do not. In light of this incontrovertible truth, in Chapter 5 Patrick Dundas from Schulte Roth & Zabel looks at the essential elements a firm must consider when developing a strategy for legal document drafting that will boost efficiency and productivity, along with lawyer satisfaction and the firm's profits.

Law firm KM succeeds when lawyers use it throughout their matters and when knowledge collection requires minimal extra work. However, matters are not static – they evolve through time. Hence, it is necessary to focus on the entire matter lifecycle to actually understand and make improvements to the underlying "assembly line" of processes and tasks. With this in mind, data-driven knowledge management and matter lifecycle management are the focus of Chapter 6. Chad Ergun from Gibson, Dunn & Crutcher outlines how matter lifecycle management can be used as a means of combining both past management experience and data analytics into an integrated decision-making approach that will enable a firm to build competitive advantage.

Part One ends with a chapter on blockchain technology. Despite its fairly recent emergence, blockchain is predicted to develop rapidly. It has the potential to revolutionize finance and business, and has future application to law firms. In the near term, as Michael Dov Nogroski from Chapman and Cutler explains in Chapter 7, blockchain has the potential to respond to key knowledge management challenges within the legal profession, including transforming contract drafting and streamlining transaction workflows. Plus, this new technology raises several legal conundrums, which are explored in this article.

Part Two opens with a case study on innovation. According to the authors of this case study, Scott Rechtschaffen and James Durham from Littler Mendelson, "a true innovation strategy envisions dramatically and comprehensively changing the way firms interact with and serve their clients". Theirs is the first in a series of case studies and they describe how Littler Mendelson has used innovation as a game-changer over the past two decades and how KM can be the foundation of a comprehensive content marketing strategy.

Case study 2 comes from Fiona Parkinson from insurance law specialist BLM who describes how the firm's KM practices have evolved during its rapid expansion. This case study describes how BLM has used KM principles to strengthen client relationships, maximize firm expertise, and increase competitiveness. She advocates the benefits of a firmwide KM strategy such as they created, which included vital information on what KM means to BLM, the benefits a streamlined KM function would bring, and the firm's plan to deliver those benefits.

In the third case study, Jennifer P. Keller from Baker, Donelson, Bearman, Caldwell & Berkowitz explains how her firm takes a holistic approach to law firm strategic planning and she offers a unique perspective on the function of KM in the pursuit of a firm's strategic goals. She outlines the steps her firm's KM team have taken to ensure their initiatives become a part of the strategic fabric of the firm, and explains how KM has moved from a traditional content generation role to a total practice management/consultancy and product development role. Jennifer provides five keys tips that have emerged as central to the success of their KM team in that context.

A final case study by David Laud from Samuel Phillips explains how the UK firm is using social media to share content, boost its brand profile, and increase connections. He explains how the firm has tackled market challenges by introducing a number of innovations with the aim of keeping the firm competitive and at the forefront of its market.

At its most basic level, knowledge management is about connecting people, functions, and systems while collecting critical knowledge artifacts, experience, and know-how for reuse or optimization. However, as the chapters and case studies in this book show, when focused on achieving business outcomes and when incorporated into the strategic fabric of a firm, KM evolves into much more. Its applications within the areas of operational efficiency, pricing, business development, marketing, and innovation are just some of the ways in which it can have measurable and profitable results for a law firm. As clients increasingly look to their law firms to add value, the right KM strategy can help a firm meet and even exceed the expectations of its clients, as well as set it apart from the competition.

About the authors

Toby Brown is the chief practice officer (and was previously the director of strategic pricing and analytics) for Akin Gump (www.akingump.com). In this role, Toby works to develop creative pricing arrangements focused on meeting clients' needs. Also in this role, he works with practice group leadership to identify and implement various efficiency-producing programs and projects, including legal project management, process improvement, practice innovation, alternative staffing, and strategic partnering.

Prior to joining Akin Gump, Toby served in similar pricing roles for both Vinson & Elkins and Fulbright & Jaworski, where he also drove knowledge management (KM) initiatives and various marketing efforts. Previously, Toby served as a director for the Utah State Bar, operating various departments, including communications, technology, continuing legal education, access to justice, and the pro bono project.

Toby presents nationally on legal pricing, law practice management, financial management, knowledge management, legal marketing and business development, alternative fee arrangements, social media marketing, and other legal market subjects. He has also published numerous articles on these topics. Toby has served on a number of legal services boards, bar association task forces, and legal market organizations. He received the Peer Excellence Award, the President's Award, and the Anne Charles Award from the National Association of Bar Executives. He maintains the ABA-award-winning *3 Geeks and a Law Blog* with two colleagues at www.geeklawblog.com.

Harriet Creamer is a corporate lawyer by training, having worked for many years at Freshfields Bruckhaus Deringer, where she became a partner. However, she has spent the majority of her career involved with knowledge management, first at Freshfields, where she was the City's first PSL before becoming partner in charge of KM, information services, and learning and development across their global network, and latterly as an independent consultant. She advises law firms in London and elsewhere on how to leverage their knowledge and experience to support more efficient working practices and drive profitability while continuing to deliver value and quality to clients.

Michael Dov Nogroski is the director of practice innovations at Chapman. He oversees the firm's knowledge management efforts and strategic initiatives to develop technology systems and processes that promote the collective knowledge of the firm, reduce risk, and increase efficiency and collaboration to the continuous benefit of firm clients. He works directly with the knowledge management partner, firm attorneys, information services, professional development, and other departments to develop the firm's knowledge strategy.

Michael combines over 20 years of technology experience with 13 years of legal experience, both as an attorney and in knowledge management. He started his career in Austin, Texas working in the technology sector and later attended law school. He has led and consulted on many complex technology initiatives, including an award-winning internal portal project. He also has extensive experience developing web-based platforms between law firms and clients that facilitate collaboration, information distribution, and matter oversight.

Michael previously worked as the team lead for the IT Business Analyst group at McDermott Will & Emery LLP and as a senior knowledge management analyst at Seyfarth Shaw LLP.

Patrick Dundas is an associate in the New York office at Schulte Roth & Zabel LLP, where he serves as the knowledge management associate for the Investment Management Group. In his role, Patrick provides the group with practice support (including advising on new issues of law affecting the private investment fund industry), knowledge brokerage services (connecting information seekers with information resources), knowledge innovation services (conceiving and developing new systems and procedures designed to increase efficiency), and knowledge management services (maintaining information repositories and overseeing compliance with internal procedures). In addition, Patrick generally serves as the liaison between attorneys and various business departments within the firm, such as the firm's information technology, marketing, and training departments, helping translate business needs into systems and procedures.

Before adopting his role as KM associate, Patrick advised hedge funds and investment advisers in connection with their structuring, formation, and ongoing operational needs, general securities laws matters, and regulatory and compliance issues.

James Durham has been one of the leading authorities on law firm marketing and business development for nearly 25 years. In that time, Jim has participated in every aspect of the legal business. After practicing business law for 10 years, he started the Law Firm Development Group, where he worked with hundreds of law firms as a consultant and trainer, developing sales, marketing, and management strategies designed to change the way lawyers and clients work together. He has interviewed hundreds of law firm clients, and spoken at dozens of retreats and conferences. Jim has been a consultant to several in-house law departments, and served as the CMBDO for three AmLaw100 firms. He was general counsel and vice president of marketing for Senior Tour Players, Inc. He also served as the senior vice president of sponsorship and affiliate relations for MLB.com. In 2010 Jim was inducted into the Legal Marketing Association Hall of Fame.

As the chief marketing and business development officer at Littler Mendelson, he is responsible for helping attract, grow, and retain clients through innovative sales and service strategies. He works closely with Littler's knowledge management department in developing and promoting innovative service solutions.

He is the author of *The Essential Little Book of Great Lawyering*, and co-editor of the American Bar Association's book *The Lawyer's Guide to Marketing Your Practice*, second edition. He wrote *The Law Firm Marketer's Guide to Survival*, and is about to complete a new book, *The Essential Little Book of Service Excellence*. For more information, see www.greatlawyeringbook.com.

Chad Ergun has 20 years' experience in the legal technology sector, and has been driven by the idea that technology should be able to offer more to the business of running a law firm and its clients. While well maintained, highly available e-mail, networks, and applications are the foundation of any legal technology department, Chad's focus has been in the area of designing data-driven knowledge management platforms, improving practice services, offering advanced e-discovery solutions, and client-facing initiatives.

Over the last 18 years, Chad has honed his expertise as he has worked to understand and build solutions across areas like knowledge management, practice support, business intelligence, e-discovery, finance, marketing, and human resources.

In his current role, Chad leads the global practice services, business intelligence, and knowledge management groups at Gibson Dunn with members in multiple locations covering practice solutions, e-discovery, business intelligence, litigation support, application development, marketing technologies, knowledge management, and desktop and web applications.

Chad holds a master's degree in information technology with a minor in industrial management and workplace psychology. He is currently working on his PhD in information management, focusing on artificial intelligence and data mining.

Mark Gould is an independent consultant, working with law firms to help them use their knowledge better to mark themselves out from the rest of the market. Before starting his consultancy in mid-2014, he spent almost 13 years at Addleshaw Goddard – first as a PSL in the firm's competition and commercial practice, then as its first head of knowledge management. Prior to that, he was a law lecturer at the University of Bristol. He blogs at http://mg3c.com/blog/, and is on Twitter as @markgould13.

Jennifer P. Keller is president and chief operating officer of Baker, Donelson, Bearman, Caldwell & Berkowitz. She is a former member of the firm's board of directors and former chair of the firm's nationally recognized labor and employment department.

As an employment litigator, Ms Keller advises clients on a wide variety of issues, including discipline and terminations, benefits issues, leave, disability accommodation, policy formulation and enforcement, and similar matters. A substantial part of her practice is providing training for employers in the areas of harassment and discrimination prevention, drug-free workplace, union avoidance, and other employment law issues. Ms Keller also has extensive appellate experience, including the briefing and argument of appeals before various state and federal appellate courts.

Licensed in Tennessee and North Carolina, Ms Keller regularly practices in both state and federal courts in those states. She also regularly appears before various administrative agencies, including the Department of Labor, EEOC, Tennessee Human Rights Commission, and NLRB. She has significant experience in mediating, arbitrating, and litigating claims based on the Civil Rights Acts, FMLA, ADA, FLSA, NLRA, ERISA, state workers' compensation laws, and state-specific employment laws.

David Laud is the chief executive of Samuel Phillips Law Firm and works with the partners to set and implement the firm's strategy. He has a varied commercial background, having held senior management positions for both Thomas Cook and AT&T. In addition to operational matters and working with business clients, he also heads the education sector, working closely with schools.

David's role sees him negotiating with suppliers and managing matters of compliance. As a chartered marketer, he has also introduced a number of initiatives that have helped to drive Samuel Phillips forward, including branding, website, and social media initiatives, and iPhone and iPad Apps.

David is regularly asked to deliver workshops and seminars on management matters, including business start-up, academies, procurement, social media, and a range of marketing related topics. He has appeared on UK national radio station Radio 4 as an expert on social media marketing, and he has two published books on the subject. This experience is often useful to Samuel Phillips' commercial clients who are seeking impartial advice to assist in growing their business.

Matt Laws is the senior director of practice management for Crowell & Moring LLP. In this role, Matt works with current clients, prospective clients, and firm partners in developing innovative value-based fee arrangements. Matt's focus on client relationships via a value-oriented approach includes legal project management and knowledge management throughout the lifecycle of engagements to ensure the effective and efficient delivery of legal services. Matt earned an MBA in finance, an MA in project management, and has 10 years of experience in managing AFA agreements at AM Law 100 firms.

Keith Lipman is a well-regarded expert in the area of information management and e-discovery, in which he has been involved for almost two decades. Prior to founding Prosperoware, Keith was the director of legal solutions at iManage, Interwoven, and Autonomy iManage. He developed the go-to-market strategy for iManage in the legal industry and was the progenitor of Matter Centric Collaboration and the electronic file in WorkSite 8. Before iManage, Keith served in a number of professional capacities, including paralegal, lawyer, IT director in a law firm, and technology consultant to law firms.

Keith earned his BA, JD, and MBA at Temple University. He is a frequent speaker and is a contributing author of the book *Corporate Governance Best Practices: Strategies for Public, Private, and Not-for-Profit Organizations*. He has also authored a number of articles on e-discovery and the management of email, documents, and records.

Fiona Parkinson is head of knowledge management at BLM, the leading risk and insurance law specialist in the UK, and for the past year has been establishing a new function, bringing together legal research services and a new team of PSLs across the firm. She has set up and managed similar functions at The Law Society of England and Wales and in energy and customer services companies, globally as well as in the UK. Her other experience includes senior roles in business analysis, information, and knowledge management in multi-national pharmaceutical and biotechnology companies, and three years with PwC.

Fiona is skilled in strategic thinking, relationship building, project management, communications, and change management. She is an effective thinker, outcome and customer focused, experienced in managing people and resources for maximum organizational advantage. She has set up and run intranets and document management systems with supporting taxonomies as well as records management and information compliance functions.

She takes a pragmatic approach to ensure KM forms part of the firm's strategy and delivers practical results to support BLM staff in their work with clients. Knowledge harvesting from projects, knowledge exit interviews, after action reviews, and expertise directories feature frequently in her KM toolkit. She believes strongly in working with marketing, IT, L&D, and HR functions to deliver joined-up solutions to lawyers and their clients.

Scott Rechtschaffen is chief knowledge officer at Littler Mendelson and leads Littler's effort to provide innovative client services by integrating new technologies and work processes and enabling attorneys and clients to access the collective knowledge and experience of the firm's more than 1,000 attorneys. He combines over 25 years of experience representing companies in every area of labor and employment law with a broad understanding of technology to help the firm's attorneys and their clients in tailoring unique solutions that enhance the firm's ability to deliver legal information and legal services to its clients.

Scott heads Littler's knowledge management department comprising dedicated KM attorneys, research specialists, and technologists. He was a member of the multi-disciplinary team that developed the award-winning Littler CaseSmart® approach to legal case management. He oversees the firm's electronic and print publications, internal KM systems, and online client subscription services.

Scott is the co-founder of ComplianceHR, an innovative joint venture launched by Littler and Neota Logic, a legal software company.

ComplianceHR leverages Littler's experience and knowledge of employment law with the power of Neota Logic's expert systems to provide a transformative suite of online compliance solutions for HR and legal professionals. In 2015, the *Financial Times* presented ComplianceHR with an award for Innovation in The Business of Law: Compliance & Technology.

For his achievements, Scott has been awarded the Distinguished Peer Award as KM Champion of the Year by the International Legal Technology Association, named to the Fastcase 50, an annual compilation "honoring the law's smartest, most courageous innovators", and was named among the 10 most innovative lawyers in North America by the *Financial Times* in 2014.

Part One:
Insights and practice

Chapter 1: Taking knowledge management to a strategic level

By Keith Lipman, progenitor of Matter Centricity and co-founder of Prosperoware, and Toby Brown, chief practice officer at Akin Gump

Single-digit growth since 2008 – with no real uptick in sight – is driving large law firms to develop parallel strategies: one focused on finding new ways to grow; and one focused on operational efficiency. This state of the industry represents an opportunity for knowledge management professionals to play a strategic role in the law firm. Once the easy steps for operational efficiency are taken, typically "right-sized" staffing models and better use of office space, firms will take a hard look at their real pain points: fee predictability and a true understanding of matter economics. For that they will need *you* (although they may not know it yet). You and your ability to leverage existing work product and share collective know how. You and your ability to connect your knowledge management strategy to your firm's core business strategies and bottom line.

It won't be easy. We're an old industry and change occurs slowly. But you *can* affect change. You *can* play a meaningful role in the firm's transition to the new reality we all do business in. And you *will* be recognized for it. Let's take a look at what you need to know to make that happen.

What you need to know about the state of the industry

How did we get here? The impact of the 2008 recession took everyone by surprise and upended the legal profession as we knew it. Law-firm clients have become increasingly "cost conscious". They're looking more closely at service specifics: Are we really spending $60,000 in legal services for a $60,000 contract? They're often turning to alternative providers in pursuit of cost efficiencies: legal process outsourcers for due diligence and third-party e-discovery companies for document review. Some clients are choosing to hire more legal staff and manage their legal work themselves, essentially using a law firm as a subcontractor instead of a prime. Demands for discounts, alternative fees, and tightly managed hourly rates are a common occurrence: anything clients deem a way to get better value is fair game.

For many law firms, these trends have created a meaningful drop in demand with everyone fighting for a share of the market. This, in turn, has made the legal services industry hypercompetitive, intensifying the imperative for fundamental change in the service models law firms employ today. Alternative fee arrangements, in particular, are under the spotlight.

News flash! Alternative fee arrangements come in many disguises

While almost all law firms have taken steps to get leaner with fewer support staff and tighter margins, many people feel their firm is not under pressure because their number of alternative fee arrangements is low. Many fail to realize that clients who are tightly managing hourly rates and the billing process are creating the equivalent of alternative fee arrangements.

Let's take a simple example of what savvy clients are doing to ensure greater bang for their buck. In a typical scenario, the client first negotiates a discount on the rates and asks the partner for a budget. Then, they tightly monitor each invoice: is there any work on here that didn't add value? Is any of this work due to inefficiencies? Is every charge within the scope of what we asked for? Are they staying within budget? The result: the matter effectively becomes an alternative fee arrangement. Based on this fact, many prefer to call alternative fee arrangements and highly discounted hourly matters "non-standard fee arrangements".

What you need to know about basic firm economics

Both standard and non-standard arrangements demand price control and a basic knowledge of firm economics. Let's look at what you need to know about profit models and profit drivers to play a more strategic role in your firm.

Like everything in our industry, how we measure profits has significantly changed. Until recently, law firm profits were built into their pricing model. The billable hour was enough to cover costs and a rising profit margin. It was easy to measure profit though a simple understanding of discount from the standard or headline rate. So long as the discount was not too much, the firm made money.

This approach worked well, and firms built a compensation system that reflected that every dollar coming in the door was a good one. No longer. A new model is emerging where profits need to be truly measured at a matter level. Two partners – each having a $5 million book of business – could have radically different levels of profitability. Today, the factors that drive margins are front and center in law firms. The most important profit drivers are rates, collected realization, productivity, and leverage.

Rates are a profit driver

Although this may be obvious, the point still needs to be made: billing rates are the core pricing structure used in the legal industry, and the level of a firm's rates is key in determining its level of profitability. As a rule of thumb, a one-point increase in rates leads to a two-point increase in profit. The reverse applies as well. In our experience, firms typically have a range of 1–3 percent increase in profit for each point of rate change. The range exists because it depends on the specific timekeepers involved and the relationship between the billing rates and the timekeepers' cost rates.

Collected realization is a profit driver

Realization is the percentage of money collected versus the standard rate. Once you have a standard rate, there are three basic factors that drive down the actual dollars collected against that rate: discounts, write-downs, and write-offs. Adding these three components together gives you total realization. The final number is important, but the three components are instructive for helping you understand what's driving a level of realization.

The impact of realization is much the same as that of rates. A 1 percent drop in realization will, on average, result in a 2 percent drop in profitability (at least it does when you are relatively close to 100 percent realization). As that realization number drops, the impact magnifies. When you approach 60–70 percent realization, it becomes infinite because you are approaching the cost-rate levels of most timekeepers. In other words, you are reaching the point where your margin goes to zero. When you pass that point, it goes to negative. At a general level, the point-of-no-return is about 67 percent. However, it can vary based on the mix of timekeepers involved in a given piece of work. Some timekeeper's cost rates can be 50 percent of billing rates; others may be closer to 80 percent.

Let's look at the components of collected realization a little more deeply:

- **Discounts.** Discounts happen when the market (in the form of our clients) tells us our prices are too high for particular pieces of work.

You might think firms should lower their prices in response to this information, but that could be a mistake. Sometimes clients shop price by the level of discounts they can get. In other words, they are not concerned with the actual price as much as they are focused on the dollar amount of the discount they can extract. Whether this is rational behavior in an economic sense is not relevant. Firms need to adjust their pricing and pricing strategies in response to the market. To counter this behavior, many firms raise their headline rate so they can provide the discount without effect.

- **Write-downs.** Write-downs are reductions from a bill before it goes to the client. This reduction signals that the firm or a partner has decided that a particular effort had no value. Examples of this include: the work is out-of-scope and the partner knows the client will not pay for it; the associate was inefficient in their work; or the associate did not understand the assignment and did the wrong thing. This becomes important as firms look for ways to lower the cost of delivering a service. By identifying recurring types of write-downs and eliminating the effort before the work is performed, a firm can lower the cost of the service.
- **Write-offs.** Write-offs are reductions requested by the client after they have seen the bill. Write-offs signal that the client did not see value in a particular effort. This may occur because the firm did not communicate the value of the effort properly, or it may just be that the work should not have been done. Note that, in some cases, write-offs are just good old-fashioned flaky clients who don't pay their bills – a cost of doing business.

Productivity is a profit driver

Productivity (aka utilization) is the number of billed hours per timekeeper. Most firms will have a benchmark productivity of 1,800 to 2,000 billable hours per year, driving an expectation of a certain baseline level of productivity. For profitability, this comes into play in cost rates.

Each timekeeper has a cost per year. There are two components of cost: compensation and overhead, commonly referred to as direct (compensation) and indirect (overhead) costs. The indirect costs are usually a hot-button issue for firms, often resulting in intense debates about where various administrative costs should be applied. Side-stepping that issue in our discussion, firms decide on reasonable numbers based on the level of the timekeepers. Partners, for instance, may have higher overhead cost allocations because they use more resources. Once a firm agrees on these costs, you divide the overall cost number by the benchmark number of hours to get a cost rate per hour.

The punch line on productivity: When productivity goes down, cost rates go up. If you have a lawyer who costs $500,000 per year working 1,900 hours, her cost is $263 per hour. If her productivity drops to 1,700 hours, her cost rate increases to $294 per hour.

The impact of cost rate changes on profit is typically half that of realization. Of course, that depends on the differential between the cost rate and the realized rate. The closer they are, the bigger the impact, and it becomes just like the point-of-no-return seen in realization.

Leverage is a profit driver

The authors often think of leverage as the "great equalizer". Leverage is the amount of non-partner work versus partner work performed or, from another angle, the percentage of partner time worked per matter or per client. We take this tangent for an important reason. Leverage is the highest-impact profit driver. When firms want to enhance their profitability, they will encourage the best use of leverage and not let low productivity promote counter-productive behavior.

The basic economic concept of leverage is that the more workers work, the more owners (partners) benefit. Workers generate the profits that pay partners. Therefore, the more work pushed down to them, the better leverage the firm has, and the more profit is generated.

Of course, caveats apply. Partner-level work should be done by a partner. The mantra here is: push work down to its lowest cost while using the appropriate labor source. This sounds obvious and reasonable. However, until recently, firms have profited from pushing work up to the highest-rate source, which was a great idea when competition was low.

Taken to a logical extreme, you could make the argument that partners should do no work to maximize profits. Technically, you would be correct. If partners spent all of their time getting business in the door, and workers provided all the effort, you would maximize profit. However, as mentioned above, partners are also workers. Clients expect the high expertise of partners to be applied to their work and, in fact, many make purchasing decisions with this in mind.

Another point to consider: partner work also generates revenue. In a situation where 25 percent of the work is performed by partners, about a third of the revenue comes from their time. The bottom-line is that work should be allocated to the right resources. Firms should make every effort to move the work down while ensuring that the timekeepers involved are constantly improving their skills and taking on higher levels of work.

A final important point on leverage: when it improves, the fees to clients go down. In other words, as work is pushed to lower-cost resources, the overall fee for a given piece of work should go down. We say "should" because this is dependent on the work being performed at competent lawyer levels. If work is pushed down to timekeepers who take too much time to complete tasks, the reasonable leverage line has been crossed. Staying on the right side of that line essentially means higher profits for firms and lower fees for clients. Truly the win-win result the market is begging for.

What you need to know about system components

Once you are grounded in basic firm economics, you need to gain an understanding of the basic components of matter coding, which will help you take knowledge management to a strategic level. When you combine your unique ability to leverage work product and know-how with an understanding of firm economics and matter coding, you'll be able to build processes and systems that help lawyers become more productive, firms more profitable, and clients more likely to come back to you. We will now introduce you to matter taxonomy, task codes, and templates. They're more interesting than they sound!

Matter taxonomy (aka collective experience)

Tracking matters, engagements, and people both internally and externally is essential to leveraging past work. Yet, until recently, most partners eschewed data at the detail level and focused on delivering the best legal work regardless of cost. Now, however, with customers applying pricing pressure, partners are scrambling to gather data that will help them analyze business opportunities, support proposal generation, and assign resources in a way that protects profitability. What they are finding is that much of the data collected during the new business intake process by admins is either inaccurate or incomplete. With the advent of legal process management, alternative fee arrangements, and matter budgeting tools, this is no longer acceptable. And here is where knowledge management professionals can step in and shine.

Strategically, a matter taxonomy gives the firm insight into business development, staffing matters, and where their profit comes from. Technology exists that will enable you to build out a matter taxonomy that allows the firm to tap into their collective experience. The challenge in the legal industry is that we do not have a cash register. In the world of retail, one person enters the critical information about a product, and every time the barcode passes the scanner, the data is captured. In the legal industry, we are dependent on people not scanners to capture the details for each matter.

In designing your taxonomy, you can capture a wide range of data. This includes core data – such as matter type, sub-type, area of law, client, and matter industry – to extended data that is dependent on the matter type or sub-type, including:

- Detail on the courts, judges, and vendors who participate in matters such as e-discovery for litigation and similar levels of detail for transactions; and
- Detail on the type of the transaction: what banks and accounting firms are involved and the size of the transaction.

The authors believe that in this approach you need to capture data in four big buckets: matter type, matter sub-type, area of law, and tags that provide additional description, such as the specific legal issues that are at stake. Key to streamlining the matter taxonomy build-out is to use technology that supports fields for multiple values, especially for tags. Multiple-value fields reduce the total number of columns required to describe matters, which streamlines the input process. Multiple-value fields are also very useful when no one category fits, such as when matters address more than one area of law.

Let's drill down now on the components of a matter taxonomy.

Matter type

Matter type is a very high-level description that groups the firm's work together into a *set* of particular processes, such as:

- *Transactions* – A set of processes where the output of the work is a contract or agreement of some kind;
- *Litigation* – An adversarial proceeding in front of a trier of facts (trial court, arbitration, hearing officer, etc.) or an appeals court;
- *Regulatory* – Working with a governmental agency to facilitate complying with a law or regulation;
- *Advisory* – Counseling the client on the risks related to certain business decisions;
- *Policy* – Lobbying on behalf of a client; and
- *Financial restructuring* – An unusually litigious process that combines both transactions and the bankruptcy process.

Matter sub-type

The matter sub-type is designed to describe the process itself rather than the subject area. In the US, the high-level process of suing in a trial court is the same no matter the venue or whether the matter involves malpractice, a contract dispute, or employment discrimination. Similarly, many regulatory processes are exactly the same. In these cases, the work can be simplified into several phases: fact gathering, drafting the form, client review, and filing. The goal here is to link the sub-type with a standard set of task codes or phases (more on this further on).

Standardizing the phases the firm uses to complete a particular type of work is advantageous in several ways in that it:

- Reduces the total number of possible phase codes used during time entry;
- Enables the comparison of phases across matters even when the subject area is different. This, in turn, enables effective pricing of matters across different subject areas; and
- Reduces the total number of selections presented to the user in the system.

Area of law

The "area of law" component of a matter taxonomy is intended to describe the legal subject area. This component of matter coding keeps the subject area relatively broad: for example, labor and employment, intellectual property, contract... Many times, the subject area may have the same name as the practice group. The area of law in the taxonomy will often require multiple values.

Tags

Tags are modifiers designed to provide additional detail as needed. As a general rule, tags will be filtered by the area-of-law selection. However, they may also be filtered by matter type or sub-type. For example, if "litigation" is selected as the matter type, "class action" may also be selected.

For each matter type, sub-type, and area of law, the practice group will need the ability to track additional fields. Here are two examples:

If the matter is litigation, you may want to track:

- Court;
- Judge;

- Demand;
- Outcome; and
- Completion phase.

If the matter addresses mergers and acquisitions, you may want to track:

- Industry of seller;
- Buy side or sell side; and
- Amount of acquisition.

Capturing the data

The matter-opening process is designed to determine whether the firm should take on the matter. Capturing this level of data during matter opening is not effective. Assistants fill out these forms, and they tend to pick the first data point on the list, or the one they use the most often. Assistants also often forget to ask for details.

A better approach is to create a process where data is captured throughout the life of the matter. The initial set of data should be collected about one week after matter opening and then on a scheduled basis, depending on the length of the matter. At a minimum, data should be collected twice: once in the beginning and once at the end of the matter. Critical data can often be gathered from other systems. For example, court data can be found in the docketing system.

Why capturing this data is important

Does this sound like too much work? Look at the payoffs listed below, and you'll better understand the strategic value of capturing this level of data:

- Allows the firm to make effective price searches to understand the effort and price associated with prior matters.
- Allows business development professionals to present the firm's collective experience in a pitch.
- Let's staff use similar matters as a starting point or precedent for new matters.
- Collects history – How many times has the firm has been in front of Judge X? How does he typically rule in a particular circumstance?

This information is valuable in pricing because it helps define scope and strategy. For example, if you can anticipate that Judge X always denies a motion to compel, you could decide not to file the motion, or you could reduce the scope of the work on these types of motions. Similarly, knowing that the judge will demand settlement before summary judgment will also signal how long the litigation will last.

- On the M&A front, when you are against firm X in a sell-side capacity, you can better forecast the key terms that will need to be negotiated and how long that typically takes.

Task codes

What's in a word? Lack of precision, often. The word "task" in the legal industry is often imprecisely used. Generally when we use it, the term "task" does not actually apply to a task in the traditional sense of the word, but to work performed during a phase or a sub-phase of a matter. Confused? Many of us are. Let's de-bunk the most common misuse of this terminology and get everyone on the same page.

The root problem dates back to the design of the ABA task codes and the Uniform Tasks Based Management System (UTMBS). The purpose of these coding systems was to enable electronic invoicing. This code set has been used primarily in the area of litigation and the cost codes around the management of expenses and disbursement.

Take the example of discovery in the ABA Litigation Code Set. The phase code for "discovery" is L300, which represents the discovery phase. The task codes include "written discovery", "document production", "depositions", "expert discovery", "discovery motions", and "other discovery". However, these labels all represent sub-phases, not tasks. The real tasks lie underneath.

Things got worse when many clients and law firms decided they didn't like the ABA labels and changed them to fit their needs. For example, the official label for L200 is "pre-trial pleadings and motions", but some clients want it to read "pleading and motions". As a result, within a single firm the same code can have slightly different meanings for different clients or for internal firm purposes.

The problem with all these codes is that a significant number of lawyers don't use them accurately. Anecdotally, we've been told on numerous occasions that as many as 60–80 percent of time entries have inaccurate codes. Much of the problem stems from the fact that there are over 29 codes in just the litigation code set. A choice of 29 codes is a lot, especially when you need to enter codes all of the time. If lawyers bill eight hours per day, they will need to make somewhere between eight and 20 time entries per day or 2,000 to 5,000 time entries per year. Whew!

Our general experience with look-up lists on frequents activities is that they should ideally number less than five entries and no more than 10. After 10, the accuracy of picking the correct selection diminishes pretty quickly. This conclusion is based on best practices that emerged from one of the author's experience designing and managing document management systems, which have exactly the same metadata problem.

While the UTMBS tasks codes are good for billing, they do not actually help you effectively price or estimate a matter. When you go back and look at a prior matter, you will find little information about critical details. In most US litigations, the critical details that make the difference in cost are the number of motions, number of documents, and number of depositions. This is next-to-impossible to ascertain because traditionally no one tracks the "real tasks" underneath the sub-phases.

To understand this better, let's turn back to the task labels that are really sub-phases, such as "document production", a sub-phase during which many specific tasks are carried out. Examples of these tasks include collecting documents, processing documents, planning for document review, reviewing documents, quality assurance regarding the reviews, and producing the documents. Some sub-phases are simpler but still problematic. For example, in the area of "depositions", you have two fundamental tasks: take a deposition and defend a deposition. These are very different things, but under e-billing they all get grouped under "depositions".

If you notice, all actual tasks start with a verb. Under each of these tasks are a multitude of activities that may be performed by different people. Let's take the example of taking a deposition:

- Schedule the deposition (secretary or paralegal);
- Pull the hot documents (associate);
- Review the documents (partner);
- Build an outline (partner);
- Take the deposition (partner); and
- Update the factual timeline (associate).

As you can see, we have three people involved in this one actual task, which means that process improvement may simply require improving the speed with which one of these activities gets done.

Measuring and getting to this level of detail is the nirvana. However, to get there, current technology is going to need to evolve, and the partners in your firm will need to agree on the list of tasks and activities in each phase and sub phase. Many practices have no task coding standard, especially for most of the transactional and regulatory matter types. Without coding standards, firms often struggle to get their practices better at pricing and delivering their services on budget. As a knowledge management professional, you can work with the partners and senior associates to establish a set of tasks codes for these matter sub-types. To do this, you will need to work with each practice group to define the phases and sub-phases of their work. The real struggle is always to balance the need for specificity with the reality of what people will actually enter in their time entries.

Templates

Pricing pressure pushes the need for templates and precedents. We live in a world where clients often will not pay for work they consider inefficient whether they are in an alternative fee arrangement or not. This creates an opportunity for you, as a knowledge management professional, to develop better templates that can be embedded into processes.

It is an easy sell: partners will recognize the efficiency of templates in terms of their impact on productivity, which we have learned is one of the factors that drive profit. Partners will also recognize the high cost of not readily finding information. Good access to information is the basis for improved decision making, it saves time and frustration, and it leads to less duplication of effort.

The value of integrating templates into your processes can be summarized in this way:

- Allows the firm to more easily push certain work down to less skilled associates, which reduces costs while improving leverage (another profit factor);
- Guides decision-making and enables legal professionals to work more effectively;
- Reduces seek time and the high cost of not readily finding information; and
- Makes appropriate documents available at the push of a button.

Netting it out

Law firms stuck in the past raise suspicions. Clients want firms that deliver high quality service at the right price. Please remember that high-paying, bet-your-business work is a perception of the client not the firm. More and more, legal services are perceived as a commodity, and clients are reluctant to sign up for services where fees cannot be projected and the work does not have to pass a litmus test.

As a result, non-standard fee arrangements have become the new normal. Non-standard arrangements come in a number of disguises, including very tight management of hourly rates and the billing process by the client. These factors all amount to the same thing: we can no longer count on profit being simply built in to the rate. Operational efficiency has become as important to law firms as growth to protect their profitability.

This chapter is a call to action for knowledge management professionals. In marketing terms, we call it increasing your brand. When you help the firm become more profit-driven by increasing operational efficiency at every level of the business, you are adding strategic value to a very high degree. And for this, your brand will morph from that of simply a resource to that of a change agent: one that helps your firm to continue to be profitable even as their market becomes very cost conscious.

Take a partner out to lunch. Describe how you visualize taking knowledge management to a strategic level. We bet the partner will pick up the bill.

Chapter 2: Utilizing KM to inform the pricing of legal services

By Matt Laws, senior director, practice management at Crowell & Moring LLP

The trend of law firms hiring pricing professionals to develop alternative fee arrangements to creatively meet the needs of corporate clients' budgetary pressures appears to have moved from a competitive advantage for firms to a strategic necessity. The impetus of this change in the legal industry is the widespread change in how clients retain legal services. This development necessitates law firms hiring pricing professionals with skill sets who understand the intricacies of various legal practices and legal engagements. These skills include budgeting for multi-year engagements, developing assumptions, and considering potential scope changes, which are all changing the way firms operate.

Historically, the negotiation between client and in-house counsel revolved around the billable hourly rate. The firm would lead with its standard rates and the client would push back asking for a discount. While this dialogue still exists today, the conversation has drastically changed and become much more advanced. Often, clients are either asking for alternative fee arrangements such as fixed fees, success fees, etc., or they are asking for hourly rates with a target legal budget so they know what to expect for the entire engagement. Firms have invested heavily in pricing departments to respond to these client demands and navigate the firm towards a path of profitability. The key requirement for the pricing professional is access to knowledge management and more specifically pricing analytics to accurately guide the firm's partners and clients.

The talent pool of pricing directors with experience, although growing, is limited and thus in high demand. Pricing directors at full-service law firms must have a significant amount of knowledge across the many practice areas and understand how the legal engagements flow through the milestone phases of the various legal services provided. The fluency and accessibility of this knowledge is important as a pricing decision is often needed quickly so that work can begin on a pressing litigation matter or time-sensitive transaction. It is easy to jump from one pricing exercise to the next without documenting the knowledge obtained, but it needs to be done and invested in, as these records formalize the experience of a pricing professional. Pricing without knowledge management is just guessing. The more sophisticated knowledge management capabilities a firm has, the more accurate their pricing will be, which leads to all kinds of benefits down the road, from the volume of work extended by clients to the very financial health of the firm. This chapter covers several methods and benefits of incorporating KM into the pricing of legal engagements for both clients and the firm.

In-house counsel and law firm partners have the common goal of arriving at an equitable fee arrangement for an engagement, which increasingly takes the form of an alternative fee arrangement. Getting to that arrangement is aided by having historical representative matters at the ready. Law firms should have, or be striving to create, an experience database of profiled historical matters and respective fees. In-house legal departments often have e-billing analytics that provide what similar matters have historically cost. This depth of financial analytics provides a solid basis for arriving at a fee agreement that can deliver predictability of legal investment via a fixed fee or assumption-based target budget, which has become the norm for engaging a law firm. The intersection between firm and client analytics is the key to arriving at an equitable fee agreement for both parties.

The role of the receptive law firm is to develop an understanding of what recent engagements cost by practice and by phase of work. This includes matter profiling the most common engagement types for each practice area organized in a firm's resource and experience database. This data needs to be cataloged in a way that is easily dissected as no two cases are exactly alike. It should be noted that this effort requires a significant investment of time and the focus should be on matter types that are common to the firm. An effective way to arrive at the most relevant matter types is to interview practice group leaders for their insight and recommendations.

The benefits of the investment include a "knowledge advantage" when pricing future engagements that arise via RFPs or informal fee quotes. A quick and thorough response is helpful to winning the engagement and avoids making the common response of, "at this early stage it is too difficult to provide an estimate of the fees". Additionally, it provides the foundation for making an informed fee quote that is not developed using estimated fees with an added risk cushion that so often eliminates a firm from serious consideration.

A sophisticated knowledge management system provides the confidence needed to quote the most aggressive price possible to win the work. Without it, one runs the risk of losing the work due to overestimating fees, or winning the work with terms unprofitable for the firm. Firms are seeing a growing number of agreements that have the potential for significant risk to the firm and without informed pricing measures; it invites a portfolio of low profit work or no work.

In concert with internal KM resources, external services such as Lex Machina provide an added dimension to firm KM data and further refine pricing accuracy. It provides additional analytics on timelines of historical cases, jurisdictions, and judges. The alternative is reviewing scheduling orders of past cases, which is not a scalable approach. Incorporating external industry data alongside firm historical experience provides an excellent logic test to pricing assumptions and can be used to fill gaps in historical data. It is important to research new external KM pricing products as the market continues to expand as Lex Machina has signaled.

In summary, legal pricing expertise is here to stay and knowledge management is the path to success in meeting client needs for alternative non-hourly pricing and predictability of legal spend. The use of an internal experience database that is detailed by phase of the engagement via matter profiling is the knowledge management investment that is required and the primary KM resource. Complementing internal KM data includes external analytics services that continue to expand to various areas of law.

Legal pricing and KM certainly has room for improvement as software solutions are limited, but pricing professionals with a vision are improvising until technology solutions help facilitate the marriage between pricing proficiency and knowledge management. At the end of the day, the better your knowledge management, the better your pricing success!

Chapter 3: Measuring the success of law firm knowledge management

By Mark Gould, founder of Mark Gould Consulting

Formal knowledge management activities have been part of law firm life for at least 30 years. Now, most of the top law firms have at least one management role containing the word "knowledge" in the title. Most also have one or more members of staff with specific responsibility for KM initiatives, and who are tasked with providing knowledge services for lawyers in specific practice groups or across the firm. Subscription services, such as Lexis PSL and Thomson Reuters' Practical Law, allow firms without the means to invest in their own resources to get access to practice manuals, precedents, checklists, and knowledge professionals.

Firms undertake a wide range of knowledge-focused activities, but they can be reduced to three primary purposes:

- Maintaining currency with the law, and reducing risk of errors;
- Improving efficiency; and
- Changing the way work is done – improving efficacy.

The first two are most common, but the third depends on the foundation that they provide.

Given the ubiquity of knowledge support in legal practice, now is a good time to ask what value knowledge management brings to the business of law. Each of the categories of knowledge activities can be measured in different ways.

The value of keeping up to date

As the law constantly changes, there has always been a need for lawyers to keep up to date with changes in the law. Increased competitive pressure on firms now means that they need to be aware of more than just the law – they need to know what new issues are affecting their clients and the sectors they operate in. Firms also monitor the legal market itself to be sure that they are working in ways that best meet their clients' needs.

Historically, firms could rely on legal publishers for information about changes in the law. This is still the case, although many firms supplement the general view provided by external providers with additional insight highlighting the impact of legal change on their own clients and sectors. Legal and other publishers will also provide information about client and sectoral issues, but this will usually require significant filtering and tailoring to avoid lawyers being overwhelmed with irrelevant material. In addition to briefings, firms will also provide training to ensure that their lawyers have a proper understanding of the law and (often) of the way the firm expects it to be used.

Given that all firms operate against this constantly shifting background, there is little or no competitive advantage in this kind of knowledge activity. However, it is possible to measure its value negatively – what would be the consequence of *not* managing this information flow properly?

In the past, some knowledge folk might have responded to a question about the value of the work they do by pointing to volumes of documents in a know-how database. All this demonstrates is the amount of work done — it doesn't help people to understand how the firm or its clients benefit. One approach to resolving this problem is to use some kind of qualitative assessment of knowledge activities. Asking people about their experience of the knowledge activities the firm undertakes will serve a double purpose — as well as indicating how successful past activities might have been, they can also suggest fruitful directions for the future.

It is also possible to assess the value of this base level of knowledge work within the firm by reference to the cost of errors avoided. Rather than using guesswork to assess this, every firm should have an understanding of the costs it incurs to ensure compliance and to rectify mistakes. Properly focused basic knowledge activities should be able to reduce some of these costs – especially if insurers, for example, can be shown how better information flows and lawyer training within the firm address the underlying causes of recurring patterns of mistakes in practice. This can in turn provide a guide for knowledge leaders in the firm to help them select the most important areas of work. As patterns of error are identified within the firm, they can be the focus of knowledge activities designed to reduce or eliminate them.

Improving law firm efficiency

The base level of knowledge management described above can only provide a safety net for the firm. Clients are entitled to expect that their lawyers understand the law and use it properly. Naturally, firms want to do more than that. What value do knowledge activities bring to legal businesses (and their clients)? This question has two facets. Most immediately, how can law firms measure the value generated by knowledge activities for themselves, possibly in comparison to other firms? Secondarily, across the sector, what difference (if any) has widespread use of knowledge management techniques made for lawyers, clients, and firms?

The base level of knowledge activities is concerned with content – information about the law and its application. This next level focuses on process and relationships. Once lawyers understand the material they have to work with, firms need to be sure that they are applying it consistently. This might be expressed as a formal process or simply as "the way we do things here". Clients also expect a degree of consistency in their relationships across firms. Some express that formally as part of their terms of business. Each of these approaches to consistency should mean that the firm can work more efficiently, as long as fee earners understand (and comply with) what is required of them. Knowledge teams support this by using tools and techniques like precedent documents, style guides, client or practice wikis, blogs, and so on.

The value of consistency in practice can be measured in the same way as core knowledge activities – by using questionnaires and quantifying error-avoidance. However, it is also possible to attempt to gauge its value in contributing positively to the firm's financial performance because consistency leads to improvements in efficiency. When working on activities to improve the efficiency of legal work in the firm, the law firm knowledge professional is aiming to extract more value from the firm's core resources. For example, standard precedent documents will shorten the time taken to produce first drafts of agreements. Other techniques and activities will have a similar impact, such as enabling work to be done by less-experienced personnel at lower cost.

If the set of things done to improve consistency and efficiency are successful (allowing for the fact that some may be more successful than others), the firm should become more productive.

The next question is how productivity might be measured in a law firm. The answer depends on whether you want to consider the firm in isolation or compare it with the market as a whole. Financial data that is available within the firm may not match what is made available for publication.

Generally speaking, productivity is an expression of the ratio of outputs to inputs. At the national level, for example, the UK Office for National Statistics derives labor productivity estimates by dividing measures of output by some measure of labor input. In professional services, productivity is measured by the turnover of companies adjusted for average wage rises in the sector.

Within a firm, inputs and outputs can be measured precisely. Firms know how many people they employ, how much they are paid, and how long they work. They also know which of these people contribute directly to the firm's turnover. Productivity could therefore be measured as a ratio of turnover per person (full-time equivalent or otherwise) or per hour worked. Such a measure would not be useful for comparison over time, since inflation might increase fees without a real increase in yield. Using the ratio of income to salaries would smooth out such variations, since inflation in fees is likely to run at a similar rate to pay inflation.

Over time, then, a firm can see how productivity changes from year to year. As law firm knowledge management efforts tend to focus on the income-generating side of the business, examining the productivity of fee earners in isolation over a significant period should help to show whether those efforts have had a real impact.

If comparison beyond the firm is needed (to check whether the firm's productivity matches changes in the market), then publicly available data sets are needed. The most easily accessible data is collected annually by *The Lawyer* (in the UK) and *The American Lawyer* (in the US). Both the Lawyer UK 200 and the AmLaw 100 calculate revenue per lawyer (RPL), which can be used as a proxy for more precise measurement of productivity. Because this measure does not take account of inflation, comparison between firms is only possible in a single year. On its own, that comparison is almost worthless. From factors such as the firm's employment profile (does it depend on low-cost associates or is it partner-heavy in high-cost locations?), its client types, or work profile, little real insight is possible. At best, firms might pick comparators they know to be broadly similar.

There is a useful way to use published figures for revenue per lawyer. That is to compare the *trend* in a firm's performance with a larger set. For example, the median RPL figure for the top 100 firms can be plotted against time. That line is likely to ascend, with occasional dips when the wider market was under stress. (It is preferable to use the median in preference to the mean in order to reduce the impact of particularly high- or low-performing firms in any given year.) When the RPL for a single firm is plotted alongside the whole set, one can see whether the profile of the line matches that for the whole set (performance in line with the market) or whether it rises more steeply (outperforming the market) or more shallowly (underperforming against the market).

This graphical information, when combined with what is known inside the firm about any special factors, allows the firm to understand better how well it is doing in the market and what might be causing any difference in performance. The special factors could include investment in knowledge activities, as well as significant client wins or losses, so some caution is still needed.

Law firm comparisons

By comparison with some enterprises, law firms derive much more value from their people. Without doing the comparative revenue per lawyer analysis described above, it is impossible to be sure that law firm productivity is not stagnant. Even if the sector as a whole looks more productive, it is possible that only a few firms stand out as particularly good performers.

The economic model of law firm operations that prevailed for most of the last century was a simple one, but it had interesting ramifications for knowledge activities. At its heart is an expectation that time spent by fee earners on chargeable work should be billed and recovered in full from clients. This emphasis on recovery imposes a burden on time-keepers to ensure that as much time as possible is attributable to client work. These two elements – recoverability and utilization – are still important to firms, but it is much less likely now than it was in the past that the effort expended by fee earners will correlate directly with income.

When firms are accustomed to high levels of recoverability, clients are the main beneficiaries of improved efficiency in legal practice, generated by knowledge activities or otherwise. Reduced time spent by fee earners to deliver the same work directly produces lower bills. Therefore, unless there are other constraints on fees, improvements in efficiency arising from knowledge management activities can have no significant impact on law firm productivity.

Since the beginning of the global economic recession in 2008 (and probably even before that), law firms have faced a continuing downward pressure on fees. One reason for law firm productivity apparently being depressed is that, although output (if measured in terms of chargeable hours worked) may be constant, clients are no longer willing to pay the headline hourly rate for that work. The need to extract maximum value from each hour worked now means that even the most basic knowledge management activities can improve law firm productivity.

When comparing law firm RPL figures over time, there may be little real change. Allowing for mergers and other major structural changes, the ranking of firms has changed little. Does this mean that there is no real productivity benefit from knowledge management activities? The answer is difficult to find. The relationship between any management intervention and productivity is murky at best.

Even if a change in practice correlates with improvements in productivity, there may be no provable causative connection. Also, most firms have adopted very similar forms of knowledge management, so that efficiencies in practice are the same across the sector. However, detailed analysis of the data may show that those firms that are falling behind have done so because of a lack of knowledge management. Most knowledge activities are easy to adopt, so they give no firm a lasting advantage.

Efficacy rather than efficiency

Real and lasting increases in productivity only arise when firms find ways to generate more income from the same amount of fee-earner work. Alternatively, continuing improvements to productivity may come from products or services that can generate income without incurring costs at the same time. These are more likely to be unique, or at least difficult to replicate, unlike efficiency-focused activities.

At present, however they resource the work that they do, most firms incur salary costs at a similar rate to the income they generate (unless they run below capacity). Firms with products or services that "make money while we sleep" (as a managing partner once described them to me) will produce income that goes straight to the bottom line once the investment costs of creating those products or services have been met.

The difference between improving efficiency and efficacy is fundamental. Efficiency is concerned with reducing the resource required to produce a particular *output*. Thus, the effort required to produce a contract for a client is reduced by the availability within the firm of standardized or automated documents and paralegal resource to carry out essential tasks that do not need significant expertise. Efficacy is more interested in the *outcome*. An efficacious result for the client who is focused on a specific business result (such as managing a group of employees) may be to provide an online toolkit to produce key documents without the firm's involvement each time.

Creating more efficacious legal services is becoming increasingly straightforward (albeit still not cheap), typically using a combination of technology and knowledge. While the technology may be available to all, the best new law firm products use knowledge that is specific to the firm. Given that new products or services of this kind are therefore more likely to differentiate firms from each other, continuing investment in improving efficacy should result in lasting productivity gains. Development of new products and services cannot generally proceed without the foundation provided by traditional knowledge activities – they usually extend the capability of existing strands of work. So, while traditional knowledge activities might add only marginal value to the firm, they are essential to the creation of real value for the firm and for clients.

Chapter 4: How KM can give clients more value

By Harriet Creamer, director at Outer Circle

Law firms increasingly sell themselves on the strength of their teams' commercial and business understanding and their ability to deliver practical yet innovative solutions to clients. Despite this, general counsel continue to complain that law firms fail to grasp the commercial realities of their business. While commercially focused promises appeal to clients, unless they are reflected in the service which is delivered (and it is provided consistently and at the right price), clients will react to them skeptically.

Ensuring everyone in the firm meets these promises is not entirely straightforward. Although most firms are reasonably good at collecting and disseminating legal and technical information, they are less effective at gathering and sharing expertise about clients and their relationships with the firm. Few firms take a truly holistic approach to managing the multiple sources of potentially valuable information, both internally and externally, which can enrich and improve client relationships.

The origins of traditional law firm knowledge management are partly to blame for the absence of this broader approach to client service. The members of the firm with explicit responsibility for KM typically focus almost exclusively on legal and technical information and standard materials. Client-related knowledge is largely outside their remit.

The KM team's engagement with client relationships is almost invariably limited to "knowledge-based" business development (producing updates and bulletins and running client seminars or, in the case of information staff, circulating news and press releases relating to individual clients and sectors to lawyers who have expressed an interest). It rarely extends to more general client relationship information.

This lack of engagement with client data is important for two reasons. First, it means that the KM techniques in which they are expert – around the collection, categorization, and retrieval of information – are not generally applied to client information, and are excluded from the firm's knowledge systems.

Second, this information is not included in the range of skills and expertise that KM professionals see as critical to building effective lawyers in the firm. This second point is particularly important if the firm's lawyers are to have the commercial and business understanding they need to deliver on its service promises.

A number of increasingly sophisticated technology-based tools are now available to help firms to surface and manipulate knowledge, and some firms are using these very imaginatively. For example, in the UK insurance sector, DWF and Weightmans are doing some very interesting work with data analytics to streamline services and present large amounts of information to clients in more manageable ways.

For those less willing or able to invest heavily, significant improvements can be achieved by explicitly acknowledging the value of expertise in managing client relationships and encouraging KM professionals to:

1. Work closely with other teams in the firm in order to identify where relevant information is held; and
2. Recognize this as something which should be shared between fee earners as a matter of course, in the same way that they share the legal, technical, and practical lessons that have been learned on individual matters.

None of this, of course, is intended to imply that it is no longer important for KM professionals to be involved in developing and supporting technical expertise in the firm. Rather, by adding client and relationship information and expertise to an excellent technical foundation, they can significantly enhance the quality of the service that your lawyers provide clients.

Practical ways to help make this a reality include:

- Setting explicit goals for both the KM and BD teams on gathering information about client relationships and transactions in relation, specifically, to commercial drivers and business needs;
- Ensuring the KM and BD functions work closely together to ensure information gathered regarding current and prospective clients is shared;

- Engaging the most experienced partners with the importance of accelerating on-the-job learning through effective off-the-job training in relation to client management, as well as legal and technical skills;
- Encouraging KM professionals to develop programs which enable senior partners to share the benefit of their experience with more junior lawyers, for example through case-study-based workshops;
- Asking KM professionals to provide more opportunities for all fee earners to share their insights into building client relationships as a matter of course (for example, through know-how sharing sessions); and
- Engaging KM professionals with business.

Engaging KM

A key first step to ensuring that client relationship data is gathered and shared – and that its significance in developing genuinely client-centric lawyers is recognized – is to engage your KM team with your business.

KM professionals should be involved in the business planning process so that they have an insight into the firm's objectives in terms of clients and areas of work. They should also have a clear understanding of the mix of transactions and advisory work and the areas in which the lawyers with whom they work spend most of their time.

While many KM professionals have a good overview of the work being done by lawyers in their practice area at any given time, they are much less likely to have a feeling for the volumes of particular types of work over time or their contributions to revenue and profit. And, while they may be able to identify the main clients in their practice area (and, in some cases, target and potential clients), they are unlikely to know volumes and profitability of work for those clients.

With this information, KM professionals are significantly better placed both to make judgments about where they should focus their efforts and to identify the mix of legal, practical, and – critically – client management skills that the firm's lawyers need.

Firms that want to derive maximum benefit from their KM professional investment both engage their KM team in business planning and ensure that KM professionals draw up KM-focused plans designed to deliver the objectives in the business plan.

KM driving BD

All law firms use developments in law and practice as a basis for making contact with clients. Different firms approach this aspect of their business differently, with some using KM professionals extensively in knowledge-based business development and others relying largely on fee earners.

Many firms go to considerable lengths to use their internal expertise as a basis for client engagement. A few are very sophisticated in the analysis they offer; for example, using big data techniques to deliver additional value to clients in specific practice areas. By interrogating high volumes of data about previous insurance claims, for example, it is possible to predict likely outcomes in new claims.

Other firms offer one-off reports and insight pieces, going to significant lengths to produce sophisticated industry analysis reports. Almost all firms produce legal bulletins and updates for email distribution and publication on their website.

It is becoming increasingly difficult for firms to differentiate themselves through their knowledge-based offerings. Although individual clients vary widely in their perceptions, surveys over the years have indicated that much "value add" in fact adds only a limited amount to relationships. In light of these findings and the level of investment required, firms that choose to go down this route need to ensure their offering stands out.

Effective use of knowledge not only helps lawyers to keep up to date, but also enables the firm to maximize returns by ensuring knowledge-based BD materials are appropriately targeted and quality is maintained.

Considerable improvements can be achieved by adopting some quite simple measures. In particular, where the firm's KM team has a good understanding of the firm's business objectives and its client relationships, it will be significantly better placed to identify and explain the likely implications of legal and market developments for clients, and to help fee earners to decide how best to bring these to clients' attention. Team members will also have the confidence to share their insights and to suggest ways in which work they are already doing internally can be leveraged externally with clients.

A final issue is to measure return on value added. Some firms are becoming more businesslike in their approach to when and how they offer additional services and have policies in place governing the circumstances under which the services should be made available. These should require regular review – for example, through client feedback and, ideally, some quantitative as well as a qualitative analysis (such as monitoring usage of helplines, rates of access to online documentation, and email opening and click-through statistics).

Work delivery support

Using KM to support work delivery has, of course, long been a central aim for many firms. However, as firms have come to terms with the reality of working in a fee-constrained and increasingly competitive environment, their approach to legal and technical knowledge management has become more client focused.

Rather than considering how KM can make life easier for the firm's lawyers, some KM teams are focusing on how KM can be used to deliver work in a way that suits each client. Firms that have introduced innovative ways of working with clients in which effective KM plays a major part include Pinsent Masons (in its deals with Balfour Beatty and E.ON) and BLP (in its managed legal service arrangements with Thames Water).

KM can help to ensure the work that is delivered meets the clients' expectations on speed and cost, without compromising on quality. A number of new techniques and approaches to traditional KM tasks are particularly important to getting this right.

Traditionally, the approach to information storage and retrieval has relied on assumptions about the information lawyers need and the sources which should be available. KM can help by undertaking a more detailed information-mapping exercise to analyze the tasks lawyers undertake and the information they need to complete them effectively. KM has expertise in looking beyond traditional technical (legal and regulatory) information and knowing how to locate market and practice-based knowledge.

KM professionals should also be encouraged to make use of financial and other client relationship data to prioritize the development of tools (including both standard materials and standardized documented processes) which enable lawyers to deliver a polished finished product efficiently to clients. Firms focused on high-volume, relatively low-margin work have for many years understood the value of streamlining processes and commoditizing work as far as possible so that it can be managed by junior staff.

Historically, firms in high-value, bespoke practice areas have been slow to recognize that they too could take a similar approach, at least to some aspects of the work they do. While almost all have adopted a process-driven approach to discovery and, increasingly, due diligence, a smaller number of firms are looking at process mapping across a much broader range of work.

Berwin Leighton Paisner, for example, has established a small central team of lawyers and technologists that focuses almost exclusively on this work. Transactions are broken down into a series of steps or phases through a process which, put simply, enables the firm to identify where systematization is possible and to establish "best practice" in the approach to each aspect of the matter. Each step or phase is then documented and underpinned with standard materials or "toolkits" which give lawyers a step-by-step guide through the relevant processes, tying each stage to budget.

Although a small number of firms are undertaking this work on a large scale and using project management techniques to improve the delivery of key matters (such as Pinsent Masons and Addleshaw Goddard), for most this will be too big a task to tackle in one hit. For these firms, the key will be to prioritize appropriately. Typically, firms will start with transaction types that are relevant to the largest number of people (ideally, where lawyers from a range of specialisms need to work efficiently together) or with areas of work under particular fee pressure.

Alongside these more innovative tools and approaches, it is important to ensure that KM is also continuing to support quality by cascading knowledge and experience down from the most senior to the most junior lawyers. Developing and introducing processes and tools which enable matters to be delegated to less-qualified staff works only where they have been appropriately trained on how to use the tools intelligently and have access to information and data that will enable them to fill in the gaps in their own experience.

Holistic approach

While there is no suggestion that traditional management of legal and technical expertise should be abandoned, some law firms such as Withers and Taylor Wessing are beginning to take a broader view of the knowledge they need to gather, analyze, and share, and they are adopting powerful new information processing and artificial intelligence technologies to search across a wide range of data sources.

This more holistic approach to knowledge within the firm, which recognizes not just the value of sharing legal and technical expertise but also of leveraging a wider range of client-related knowledge, promotes the development of lawyers who are not only technically excellent, but are also truly client focused.

CASE STUDY

Institutionalizing key client relationships

Firm A was aware of a number of issues facing its charities practice. The team was led by an experienced partner who had built most of the key client relationships, but who was planning to retire at the end of the year. The remaining lawyers in the team included one other partner and two experienced associates who relied heavily on the head of the group for his expertise, not only on relevant law and practice but also on the preferences and backgrounds of key clients. The firm needed to be able to sustain this practice and enable it to grow after he retired.

In consultation with its KM professionals and information team (and alongside discussions with individual clients about the formal handover of each of the retiring partner's client relationships), the firm took the following steps to mitigate the risks associated with the retirement and to ensure that the implicit knowledge and expertise the partner had built up was retained in the firm and would continue to inform its relationships with his clients:

- A KM professional arranged for a trainee to conduct a series of interviews with the retiring partner, each covering a key aspect of charities law and practice, during which the partner "downloaded" his thoughts on the main issues – legal and regulatory, but also crucially the soft issues which informed the way he dealt with different types of charitable clients, his relationships with key regulators, and the commercial and practical context of work in the charities sphere. These interviews were written up into a series of short "how-to" briefs, with legal, technical, and practical/contextual sections giving simple guidance. This information was then stored in a digital handbook, which was accessible across the department.
- The trainee spent time with the partner identifying good examples, from the many matters on which the partner had worked, of core documents which were then collected together, indexed, and made available internally.
- A series of workshops were arranged at which the partner led discussions on different aspects of charities work. While key areas of law and regulation were identified during these sessions, the main focus was on their practical impact and the commercial context in which they operated.
- A member of the business development team interviewed the partner about his key clients, ensuring that critical information about his relationships with them was captured. This information was recorded appropriately on the client database and then shared with the remaining lawyers in the team.

CASE STUDY

Creating thought-leadership content

Firm B was looking at ways to maintain the pre-eminence of its banking practice. It decided to engage consultants to help it to deliver a high-quality thought leadership campaign which would appeal to its banking clients and reinforce their existing perceptions of the quality and commerciality of its lawyers.

It began by asking its banking KM professional – in consultation with banking partners – to draw up a list of the most significant issues or developments facing its banking clients. A series of workshops were then held with partners at which these ideas were discussed and a short list of topics, prioritized in order of perceived importance, was drawn up.

This list was then tested with a number of existing and potential clients of the firm. The final choice of topic for the campaign was made based on these discussions, which also helped to shape the scope and focus of the campaign.

In discussion with the banking KM professional and the firm's business development team, several key aspects were identified on which quantitative research was required, which was conducted by their team of business information analysts. The results of this research were analyzed and presented in the report which formed the core of the campaign.

The combined team then identified those clients most likely to be affected by the issues covered in the campaign, and therefore most likely to be interested and to respond positively. These clients were the core targets of the campaign.

A report was produced that drew on expertise from across the firm by practice and sector as well as geographic location, in order to showcase the firm's capability to the greatest possible extent. The report was practically focused; as well as including high-level thinking, all who contributed to it were asked to identify at least one practical impact on which action was likely to be required to highlight to clients.

The report was launched at a presentation to the core target list of clients and released to the press. Detailed roundtable follow-up sessions were offered to these clients. A series of more general client seminars were also held, based on the report, and workshops and presentations were organized internally.

Engaging KM professionals with your business strategy

- Ensure the practice/sector group and firm-wide business strategy is shared with your KM professionals so that they can identify/comment on likely knowledge needs;
- Involve KM professionals in discussions at partner level in their practice/sector so that they can match efforts to the division's priorities;
- Share financial and other data about matters and clients with KM professionals so that they can see where focused intervention (for example, increasing efficiency by providing practical tools to lawyers in areas under fee pressure) is most needed; and
- Share information on current pitches and new business with KM professionals so that they can assess likely current and future needs for KM support.

A version of this article first appeared in Managing Partner *magazine in August 2015.*

Chapter 5:

Legal document drafting – Tools and practices that enhance a firm's competitive edge

By Patrick Dundas, associate at Schulte Roth & Zabel LLP

In many legal practices, a significant portion of attorney time is spent drafting documents. If an attorney spends this time efficiently – for example, by starting with an appropriate precedent or form, or by using a document assembly program, and finishing off the draft by utilizing expert drafting skills developed over years of practice – the end result is a high-value, high-quality document. Conversely, if the attorney does not have access to precedents, forms, or document assembly programs and lacks basic drafting skills, the end result may be a low-value, low-quality document that the client over pays for and exposes the law firm and the client to risk. A well-articulated document drafting strategy, prepared and executed by a firm's knowledge management department in collaboration with others, can set a firm on the right path by providing attorneys with the tools necessary to prepare outstanding documents, while increasing the firm's profit and improving attorney satisfaction. This chapter describes several elements that every law firm must consider when developing such a strategy.

Drafting as a product: Alignment of business strategy with document strategy

Law firms provide services to their clients in connection with disputes (such as civil and criminal cases), deals (such as mergers and acquisitions), entity formations (such as start-up businesses and investment products), regulatory advice, and dozens of other categories of legal services. One may think of legal services as falling into one of the following three major categories: (i) legal research, analysis, and advice (which may be dispensed orally or in writing); (ii) persuasion (such as negotiating a deal or preparing a brief for a litigation); and (iii) drafting agreements and similar written work. Each of these categories depends heavily on written work product. In many instances, the written work can be thought of as the product that the client is purchasing, which presents the question: are there steps law firms can take to improve the quality of the product, reduce risk to the client and the firm related to the product (for example, due to product defects), reduce the cost of production, and generally increase the skills of the drafters?

Of course, the answer to this question is yes. Knowledge management personnel typically lead or collaborate with members of other law firm business departments on reaching these goals. However, taking the steps necessary to achieve these goals requires an investment of capital and internal resources, which could be significant depending on a firm's strategy. To improve document drafting, a firm may invest in training its attorneys to be better drafters, in document management systems (DMSs) and search engines, or in form documents or document assembly platforms. The more a firm invests, the better the product is likely to be (thereby decreasing risk to the client and the firm). However, as a firm gets better and faster at preparing documents, the less clients will have to pay for the product (assuming the firm bills by the hour). For some firms, this is a necessary and desired outcome – which could result in increased market share and increased profit. For others, it may be a threat (or perceived threat) to growing revenue. Every firm must determine what its long-term business strategy is and align its document strategy with the business strategy. A firm that does not risks investing in projects that are unnecessary or unwanted, or not investing in projects that are essential for the proper execution of its business strategy.

Amount of investment vs. cost of drafting

The level of investment (of capital or internal resources) varies depending on a firm's needs. When it comes to an investment in document drafting resources, there are four basic categories of investment: development of custom drafting skills, precedent management and location, form development, and document automation. The lower the investment in knowledge management tools, such as precedent search and form development, the more human labor is required to prepare a given document, which results in a higher cost of legal service to the client. This relationship is illustrated in Figure 1.

- **Level 1: Custom drafting** – An investment in developing the custom, or "bespoke" drafting skills of attorneys is required from all law firms. These skills are fundamental to the practice of law and are always needed, regardless of what other tools are provided by the firm.

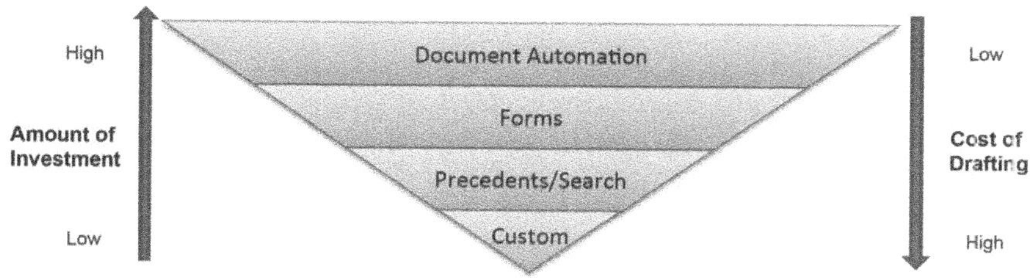

Figure 1: Amount of investment vs. cost of drafting

- **Level 2: Precedent management and location** – Once a firm has written work product, it can be reused. However, giving attorneys the necessary tools to locate the right precedent at the right time requires an investment in information technology infrastructure, and training the attorneys how to properly use the tools available.
- **Level 3: Forms** – When a firm expects to prepare the same kind of document repeatedly it should consider developing a form. Form documents require a significant amount of attorney time, but when done properly they provide extraordinary benefits to the firm and clients alike.
- **Level 4: Document automation** – When a document or suite of documents needs to be prepared in the most cost-effective manner, a document automation program should be used. A prerequisite to investing in document automation technology is having mature, well-tested forms. Given the significant amount of attorney time required to develop forms, capital required to purchase the technology platform, and attorney (and often consultant) time required to convert the forms into coded templates the platform can assemble, an investment in a document automation program can be the most expensive of all document drafting-related investments.

Custom drafting

A blank sheet of paper lies before an attorney tasked with preparing an agreement. If the firm for which the attorney works has made no investment in a precedent bank, model forms, or a document automation program, the attorney's experience and education are the only resources from which the attorney can draw to begin drafting. Of course, this scenario rarely occurs in practice; often attorneys begin drafting from precedents, whether the assignment involves persuasive writing (such as when preparing a brief for a litigation) or contract drafting. Nevertheless, drafting skills are basic skills of the trade that every lawyer must master, as they are required regardless of the drafting tools available. Even documents based on precedents or documents assembled on an automated basis often require custom alterations to meet the needs of a particular client.

Professional development investment

Though most law schools require students to take persuasive writing courses, many do not require aspiring lawyers to study contract drafting at all. As a result, most attorneys learn how to draft contracts on the job through a combination of mentoring from other attorneys, self-teaching, and continuing legal education (CLE) classes that enhance their basic writing skills. Law firms that have professional development departments should focus significant resources on making sure junior attorneys have these resources available. In the absence of these resources, the product of the firm will likely suffer.

Mentoring

Mentoring can take many shapes at law firms. Law firm partners and other senior attorneys should spend time training junior associates one-on-one during the course of a legal project, as is always necessary, but a mentoring program should include additional mentoring opportunities. For example, office sharing and informal team lunches can provide learning opportunities. Finally, knowledge management practice support lawyers (KM PSLs) can be especially useful. When performing well, KM PSLs serve as the go-to attorney to answer any questions junior attorneys have. This is especially useful for those junior associates that are nervous about asking "stupid" questions of superiors who will review their performance at the end of the year. Thus, the KM PSL can serve as the mentor and counsel to the practice group, accelerating drafting and substantive legal skills of the junior associates and raising the caliber of the group generally.

Self-teaching

While an essential component of professional development, mentoring cannot replace self-teaching. The challenge of self-teaching is that clients are not interested in paying for it and junior attorneys often do not have the time to engage deeply in self-teaching exercises. Nevertheless, it must be done. When mentoring, or providing legal advice to junior associates, senior attorneys should encourage the junior to not just take the senior attorney's advice, but to confirm the accuracy of the advice by reading primary and secondary sources. When it comes to drafting, there are several reference works that all attorneys should have at arm's length, including legal dictionaries (such as *Black's Law Dictionary* and *Garner's Dictionary of Legal Usage*) and style manuals (such as *The Chicago Manual of Style*, *A Manual of Style for Contract Drafting* (Kenneth A. Adams), *The Redbook: A Manual on Legal Style* (Bryan A. Garner), and *Typography for Lawyers* (Matthew Butterick)). By supporting and promoting self-teaching, firms can accelerate the skills of junior attorneys and improve their products.

CLE programs

Finally, CLE programs that focus on legal drafting skills should be offered regularly, especially to junior attorneys. These can be taught by internal attorneys or outside experts. Internally developed courses should focus on how to draft specific kinds of documents that are common to a particular practice, while courses that teach general drafting skills should be taught by outside experts.

Technology investment

There are several classes of technology products (in addition to word processing programs, such as Microsoft Word) designed to support legal document drafting. The most commonly used technology products are briefly described below.

Document comparison

Every law firm should have a document comparison tool, which enables attorneys to compare one version of a document to another, or any selection of text to another. The most commonly used products are Microsoft Word (native comparison function and track changes), Litéra ChangePro, DocsCorp compareDocs, Esquire iRedline, Microsystems DocXtools Compare, and Workshare Compare DeltaView.

Proofreading

There are several products that use logic to analyze the writing within a document and detect common drafting errors (for example, defined terms that are not used, capitalized terms that are not defined, numbered items that are not in order or are missing items, incorrect internal cross references, etc.). Logic-based proofreading technologies have matured in recent years to the point where they should be seriously considered as a must-have investment of any law firm. However, many lawyers are hesitant to use proofreading technologies. A successful deployment of any proofreading technology will likely depend on support from the top of the firm and a strong promotional effort. Even then, adoption can be a challenge, despite the benefits proofreading technologies bring. Several commonly used proofreading products include Microsystems EagleEye, Thomson Reuters Deal Proof, WordRake, and XRef.

Precedent management and location

Imagine a newly minted solo practitioner who has just negotiated and drafted their first contract following dozens of hours of negotiation and rewrites. Though they spent a significant amount of time (and the client spent a significant amount of money) on this contract, the next time the practitioner is asked to draft a similar agreement, they will spend less time (and the client will spend less money) if they begin with the last client's contract as an example.

This practice of reusing past work product, or "precedent", is used by lawyers to reduce the cost of their services and improve the quality of the work, among other things. The challenge for law firms is providing lawyers with tools that enable them to find the right precedent when they need it. Several tools may be made available, including curated precedent repositories, search engines that enable searching for documents by matter/party and document classification, and mechanisms to support the sending and searching of requests for information/precedent. Each practice group within a law firm should determine which of these tools best fits its culture, needs, and budget, with a combination of several tools often providing the best solution.

Precedent repositories

Many law firms employ KM PSLs who are tasked with identifying and storing documents that are considered to include the "latest and greatest" language for a given type of legal project. These are different from forms in that they are not "fill in the blank" documents, but examples of how certain clients (and attorneys) have crafted their documents. Collections of these documents may be organized in DMSs or simple folder structures in shared computer hard drives.

Precedent repositories are attractive to many law firms mainly because they appear to require a lower investment than, for example, developing forms; all that needs to be done is to put the "latest and greatest" document into the precedent folder. However, many precedent collections fail because they are not maintained over time. It is very common for a practice group to assemble a collection of what the partners consider to be the gold standard documents today, only to leave the collection sitting for years until it comprises only what used to be cutting edge.

Any precedent repository must be actively maintained, which typically requires regular involvement by support staff (such as KM PSLs) and practice group leaders. However, even with proper resource allocation and management buy in, precedent repositories are extremely difficult to keep current. This is because the "latest and greatest" documents change daily in many practices, and support teams are always one step behind.

Matter/party classification

When seeking precedent for a given document or group of documents, an attorney is nearly always seeking such documents in the context of working on a particular matter or providing services to a particular party. Accordingly, searching based on the attributes of the matter or party will often lead the attorney to the right precedent.

To be able to perform such a search, the search engine must have connections established between documents and matters and parties, and these need to be classified properly. This is no small task. Indeed, few law firms have been able to thoroughly tackle matter/party classification. Nevertheless, matter and party classification presents law firms with rewards far beyond the ability to search for precedents. For example, it supports marketing and business development, conflicts clearance, accounting, and legal project management (including pricing). By comparison, efforts to maintain precedent repositories benefit only knowledge management efforts.

A detailed discussion of how to develop matter and party taxonomies is beyond the scope of this chapter; however, given the broad benefit a successful matter and party classification initiative would provide to a law firm, if resources permit, such an initiative should be considered by all firms (and would likely be a better investment than a precedent repository).

Document management systems and search

The most efficient and effective mechanism an attorney can use to locate precedent is a DMS, combined with a strong search engine. In the modern law firm, a DMS should serve as the repository of record for all attorney working documents (that is, all documents prepared by the law firm for its clients). Many firms expand the scope of the DMS to include emails and other electronic records (e.g. PDF versions of executed agreements) due to the scalability, the technological maturity, and the security features typical of a DMS. As a result, the DMS serves as a significant resource for knowledge management purposes (precedent location), as well as records management.

Of course, a repository is of little use if its contents cannot be searched effectively, and there are certainly many law firms that have made a sizable investment in a DMS without also establishing procedures and installing a search engine that facilitate precedent location. To take full advantage of the information within a DMS, firms should develop and enforce standard document naming conventions and document type taxonomy, and implement a document search engine.

Document naming convention

Saving document files so the file name includes words and phrases that describe the contents of the document is fundamental to storing files and benefits internal users (attorneys) and external users (clients). A proper file name enables users to more quickly find a document and sort the results once they are found. Finally, a consistent and logical file naming standard simply looks nicer than inconsistent and sloppy file names. The test is always, will a person who knows little about the project/document be able to find the file?

The challenge to establishing a firm-wide document naming convention is that different practice groups may have different preferences. This challenge can be overcome by establishing a different document naming standard for each practice group. Multiple standards will interfere with the sorting of documents, but not searching, so long as all document names include the following key components: (1) a description of the type of document; (2) the parties related to the document; (3) the date related to the document; and (4) a description of the status of the file.

As noted above, the order of these components is irrelevant for search purposes; however, the order should be consistent if users expect to sort the files based on any particular component. Regardless of which file naming standard is used by a given practice group, the standard is only useful to the extent that it is used consistently across the practice, so user training is essential to adoption.

Some examples of good document file names are as follows:

- POA – John T. Smith – January 3, 2016 – Executed
- LPA – ABC Partners, L.P. – March 2, 2016 – Final
- 2016–11–03 – Jones vs Smith – Motion for Summary Judgment – Filed
- Term Sheet – XYZ Transaction – Draft

Detailed descriptions of the components of a file name are set forth below:

- **Document type** – The document type description that is included in the document name could be a full description of the document (e.g. Private Placement Memorandum; Power of Attorney) or an abbreviation of the full description (e.g. PPM; POA). Depending on the context and the established practice among a group of attorneys, either approach works, though often document type abbreviations are preferred because they result in shorter file names.
- **Parties** – Similarly, the party descriptions could be the full name of each party or an abbreviation. However, in this case, the full legal name is much preferred over any abbreviation, as abbreviations of party names almost always hinder search. Consider the following two file names, "POA – John T. Smith – January 3, 2016 – Executed" and "POA – JTS – January 3, 2016 – Executed". A user searching for John Smith's power of attorney will probably not know, unless they personally worked on the document, that the best search term is "JTS" and not the words "John" and "Smith".
- **Date** – Whenever a date would be a useful term for searching or displaying a document among search results, it should be included in the file name. This is typically the case with final versions of documents (whether a working document or final PDF version). As with the other file name components, the formatting of the date information varies. Some prefer year/month/day (e.g. 2016–01–03), some prefer writing out the date, which could be done in several different ways (e.g. January 3, 2016; 3 January 2016). The choice of format will depend on the sorting and searching needs of the users. For example, if the users will not need to sort files by date, but do expect to search by month and year, writing out the month may be useful. On the other hand, if the users will need to sort by date, the date should be expressed numerically (e.g. 2016–01–03) and the date information should start the file name.
- **Status** – If a file version is the final version or a PDF of an agreement is a scan of a fully executed copy, it should be made clear in the file name. Typically, this is done by simply including the words "final" or "executed" in the file name.

Document categorization

A universal feature of DMSs is the ability to add additional metadata to a given document. Among these metadata, the "document type" field is especially useful for precedent location purposes. Traditionally, document classification has been achieved manually by the attorney that saves the document by either assigning a specific document type (e.g. Power of Attorney) or saving the document to a folder in the DMS that automatically assigns the document type. Both of these approaches have shown to be subject to significant user error (or inattention). Most DMSs require the user to spend 5–10 seconds determining the document type. Unfortunately for data enthusiasts, most attorneys are not interested in spending any time categorizing documents and, rather than finding the proper type or folder, will save all documents under a generic document type (e.g. "doc").

In response to cultural obstacles to properly categorizing documents, some industry consultants and law firms suggest doing away altogether with document categories. This may be acceptable in a minority of firms, but the vast majority of law firms continue to find value in categorizing documents, despite the uphill battle to convince some attorneys that it is worth their time.

Though generally unexplored in the legal industry, there are technologies available that could enable firms to automatically classify DMS content; however, deploying such a technology would require a significant investment in developing a document type taxonomy and creating logic that matches document types to documents that meet a set of criteria. Few firms have shown an interest in this approach, though it is likely the most cost-effective solution to the problem of poor document classification.

Document search

Once documents are properly named and categorized in a DMS, users have two basic ways to locate them: browse folders or search for documents. Browsing folders may be an acceptable way to locate a suite of documents curated under a client or matter, but when locating precedent, it is no substitute for search. Without a sophisticated search engine that allows for full text Boolean searching of document names and the full text of documents and the filtering of results based on metadata (such as the document type), the utility of the DMS is significantly impaired.

For reference, the following are DMS products, matter/party classification products, and search technologies that are commonly used by law firms: Autonomy Universal Search; BA Insight; HubbardOne Experience Manager; iManage; IntApp; Lexis Search Advantage; Lexis

Total Search; MatterSphere; Microsoft (SharePoint; Matter Center); NetDocuments; OpenText/Hummingbird; ProLaw; Recommind; West km; and Worldox.

Requests for information/precedent

The final precedent location tool is one that is commonly derided but nevertheless essential for most firms. It is the "request for information" (RFI) or "request for precedent" (RFP) message. Often manifesting themselves as emails sent, completely untargeted, to the entire firm or practice group, in the worst case scenario, these emails pose questions with such obvious answers that many recipients cringe at the ignorance of their colleagues, with some taking it upon themselves to privately or publicly let the sender know how ill-advised and unnecessary the email was. Many view RFI/RFPs as a source of distraction and lost productivity, and as producing little actionable intelligence.

However, no matter the sophistication of a firm's knowledge management function, there is always a need for some kind of ad hoc knowledge-gathering mechanism. This need could be satisfied by an email system, an electronic bulletin board, a social media platform, or any other technology, so long as the platform enables information seekers to connect with information holders and memorializes the event and the information sought and found so other attorneys can search and find the information without sending a similar, duplicative request.

When used appropriately, an RFI/RFP is sent only after all other methods of information location have been exhausted, is stored in a searchable repository, and is tagged with the identity of the sender and the client/matter number (but not client or matter names to protect confidentiality in the event that ethical walls are applied to the client or matter). It is crucial that these requests include the name of the sender and the client/matter number so that when the request is found later by an attorney, that attorney knows whom to contact and what client/matter number might hold information of interest.

Forms

Many practices operate well relying solely on precedents. However, if a practice finds that it is drafting the same documents repeatedly and frequently, it should explore whether these documents should be made into forms. Using forms improves the quality and consistency of the product, reduces risk to the client and the firm, increases efficiency, accelerates associate training, and supports increased leverage, as more fully described below.

Quality and consistency

A law firm's brand is based in large part on the quality and consistency of the documents that it produces. Maintaining this quality and consistency can be a challenge if a firm relies only on precedent when preparing documents because precedents evolve over time. Every time a precedent is reused for a new client, the drafting attorney and the client, and often opposing counsel, make edits, for better or worse, that result in diversity. Over time, a firm could have dozens of different examples of the same document type, all with minor variations based on a particular client's needs. Some of these variations will be substantive differences and required, but others will be only stylistic variations. A firm that synthesizes the variations among precedents into a suite of form documents that have a consistent style and take into account the majority of possible client conditions will be able to produce documents that have a consistent look and feel, and maintain the substantive quality of the original precedents. (For a technology product that supports the creation of forms, see KMStandards.)

Risk

Without a single authoritative source for a given document, associates prepare documents based on precedent that may or may not include every provision appropriate under the circumstances. This increases the risk that the firm's product has a material defect. Well-maintained standard forms reduce this risk. Though most forms cannot include all possible permutations, they often can include provisions that cover the most commonly encountered client needs, thereby greatly reducing the risk that a document will be drafted without an essential component.

Efficiency

Though attorneys generally do not like to analogize the business of law to other businesses, there are lessons to be learned and processes to be borrowed from non-service industries. The advisory services provided by attorneys are labor-intensive exercises that are difficult to make less so, but the labor required to prepare many documents can be reduced by replicating processing pioneered and perfected by the manufacturing industry. Standard forms make this efficiency possible.

There are several ways form documents increase efficiency. First, finding a standard form requires less time than researching which precedent to use. Second, it often takes less time to draft based on a form than it does to draft based on a precedent. The pace of drafting is not only increased because the form generally includes all the necessary instructions and language for an attorney to complete the draft, but over time attorneys become familiar with the form so that time need not be spent reading every word of the document every time – once an attorney has drafted 50 of the same document based on the same form, they need only review the variations. Third and finally, knowledge embedded within forms as annotations and drafting instructions accelerates attorney training, resulting in more knowledgeable attorneys who are able to respond to client questions with less research, as discussed below.

Training and leverage

Perhaps the most valuable function of standard forms is that of a training resource, which accelerates an attorney's skill level, and therefore allows partners to delegate work to associates with less partner support. Indeed, an attorney should be able to draft a document based on a form with no previous training at all. All the information necessary to draft (other than the facts applicable to the related parties) should be embedded within the form. This information can be classified under two categories: drafting instructions and annotations.

Drafting instructions are often included in form documents as footnotes and explain to the drafter how to draft a particular provision or which sample language is appropriate to use under a certain set of factual circumstances. Think of drafting instructions as the "how" of the form. Annotations are the "why" of the form. The best annotations clearly and concisely explain why a form works the way it does or why certain language is in the form at all. When appropriate, citations to primary sources (e.g. laws, regulations, cases, etc.) and secondary sources (e.g. memos, treatises, etc.) should be included. To clearly differentiate drafting instructions from annotations, annotations may be embedded within the document as "comments" in Microsoft Word.

Finally, and most importantly from a business perspective, to the extent that an associate can use a form to draft a document without partner guidance, the firm can increase its leverage ratio (that is, the ratio of associates to partners), which in turn may have a positive effect on the profit per partner of the firm.

Storage of form documents

The best place to store form documents is in a DMS. In the DMS, a form document can be tagged as a form and categorized by document type for easy retrieval. It may be secured so it may be edited only by a limited group of users (or, if the form is restricted for use by a limited amount of users, viewed only by a limited group of users), and new versions of the form may be stored together so that the evolution of the form may be tracked over time. In some practices, the ability to track the evolution of a form by running blacklines of newer versions against older versions may be crucial for training and client service purposes. For these reasons, storing forms on a shared drive in a simple folder structure or presenting them solely as links in an intranet page may result in missed opportunities.

Sources of form documents

There are three sources of forms in law firms: laws and regulations (statutory forms); third-party information platforms (commercially developed forms); and in-house developed forms.

Statutory forms

Many laws and regulations prescribe specific forms to be used for compliance or other purposes. In addition, many governmental agencies produce their own forms to, among other things, improve the efficiency of their operations. Some examples include powers of attorney, healthcare proxies, and certificates of formation, among others. These forms are typically publicly available. Law firms may use these forms as the basis for internally developed forms, supplementing the statutory forms with instructional footnotes and annotations.

Commercially developed forms

There are several companies that offer forms to the public (or to law firm subscribers) for a fee. The products these companies offer are particularly attractive to law firms that do not have the resources to develop forms on their own. For firms that have developed an expertise in a particular practice area, however, commercially available forms are often seen as inferior to the in-house forms that include years of in-house experience and knowledge.

In-house developed forms

Many practitioners view their in-house forms as superior to forms from other sources, and with good reason. When done well, these forms reflect years, perhaps decades, of legal experience and are tailored to the firm's particular practice and workflows, accelerating associate training and enhancing the firm's leverage and profit. However, in-house forms are no small investment.

Form development projects are easy to begin, but extremely difficult to finish. It is not uncommon for a form project to begin with enthusiasm, but to fail because, for example, client work diverts resources from developing the form. Obstacles abound. While one partner may be a champion of a form project, another – for example, an expert whose input is essential to the success of the project – may view the form as a threat to their value to the firm and a threat to high billable hours (after all, efficiency may lead to lower billable hours, which is perceived by many as the source of profit). As described in detail below, a form project has a higher likelihood of success if there is a lawyer dedicated to leading the project (who typically is also the primary drafter), the project has support from management and involves the entire practice group, and resources are dedicated to maintaining the form over time.

Managing an in-house form development project

Form projects vary in scope from simple to extremely complicated. As a result, the workflows and teams required to support a form project vary depending on the nature of the project, available resources (human and financial), and the culture of the firm. For the sake of concision, below is one example of how a team could support a form project, but other structures could be used.

Team structure

At the heart of the form project team is the project leader. This is the person that will manage the project by doing the bulk of the drafting and coordinating contributions from the partner leader, users (that is, attorneys that use the form(s)), internal experts (if necessary), external experts (if necessary), and clients (to the extent that clients provide feedback to the attorneys). The partner leader is the primary person at the partner level responsible for reviewing and approving the form(s). This person may defer certain questions or issues of law to the practice committee, or to internal or external experts, and the authority to approve any element of a form may be centralized or decentralized, as discussed in greater detail below. This structure is illustrated in the diagram in Figure 2.

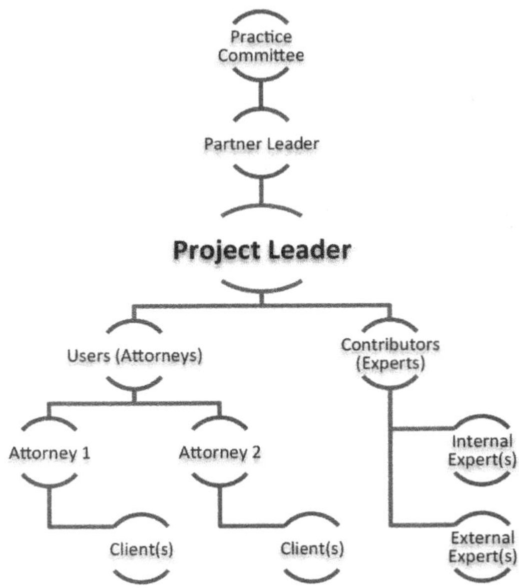

Figure 2: Form project team structure

Dedicated project leader

The leader of a form project should generally not also be servicing clients, should be an experienced attorney who is dedicated to forms and other knowledge management projects, and should be a highly skilled drafter, collaborator, and sales person with good social and political standing that has an entrepreneurial spirit.

Developing even a simple form requires several hours of attorney time at multiple levels of the organization (i.e. junior associate level, partner level, and practice group leader level). If the project involves multiple related forms, hundreds of hours of attorney time could be necessary to finish the job. As with any project, forms projects need a point person: a project leader that has time to sell the project to contributors/collaborators and practice group leaders, do the initial drafting, discover drafting issues, and resolve open questions that arise during the course of the project. If the project leader is regularly pulled away for client projects, the form project will likely fail from lack of leadership and inattention.

The project leader should be an attorney with expert drafting skills and excellent collaboration skills and solid social and political standing. Accordingly, staffing a non-lawyer or junior associate as the leader on a form project will likely not result in the best outcome. A junior likely does not have the drafting skills necessary to produce the best product and also will likely not have the skills to collaborate effectively with other members of the team (who are often partners) to whom the project leader may be averse. If a supervising partner provides poorly drafted comments to a form that is inconsistent in style or substance to the form as a whole, a junior associate might not have the skills to improve and harmonize it with the rest of the form and might not feel comfortable correcting any errors of a superior. For these reasons, well-seasoned attorneys are usually the best choice to lead form projects.

Finally, the form project leader should have an imaginative, entrepreneurial spirit and the grit and tenacity to push the project forward against possibly apathetic and oppositional collaborators. Every form project will encounter obstacles, and the project leader needs to be able to manage the project to overcome them.

Authority

The authority to approve final language within a form runs on a spectrum between centralized and decentralized. In theory, the authority to approve a final form should always be entirely centralized. With one partner or a committee of partners serving as gatekeepers for the quality of all language in all forms, consistency and quality may be ensured. Firm-approved forms are designated as such by the leaders of the firm and users may rely unequivocally on the language as the "latest and greatest" available. However, in practice, the more centralized the authority is, the more likely the project will fail due to bottlenecks in the review and approval process. It is extremely common for forms projects to fail for this reason.

Decentralization, while often more practical, is not without its own risks. Under this model, each form is best thought of as a group or firm-wide product. It is not the result of decisions made exclusively by the leaders of the firm, but is a crowd-sourced document, evolving based on the feedback of associates, partners, and clients. Each edit certainly must be subject to some level of review, but not every edit needs attention from the top. Certain edits may be approved by designated contributors, others by the project leader, with only those that are worthy of escalation brought to the attention of the practice committee. Every attorney is encouraged to use the form, but to view its contents skeptically and as a document in a state of continual evolution; to engage actively with the forms, and not passively rely on them. The more decentralized the approval process, the greater the risk that some imperfections (or at least perceived imperfections) will creep into the forms. However, this risk may be managed and mitigated by the diligence of the project leader. In addition, with adequate partner review of any work product based on the forms, any imperfections may be detected and corrected.

Management, practice group, and firm-wide support

A form should be thought of as a product of the firm, not of one person. The best forms are a result of collaboration among firm management, practice group leaders, subject matter specialists, and clients. Attorneys should be able to rely on forms, but they should never rely blindly. Each person that uses a form should be encouraged to review it critically and bring improvements to the attention of the project leader. Ultimately, clients choose counsel partly because of the relationship partner, and partly because of the team assembled behind the relationship partner, and the expectation of many clients is that the expertise of the firm is brought to bear on their legal projects. Forms are an excellent mechanism for harnessing that collective expertise.

Maintenance

Forms are never final. As the law, drafting style, typography, and language evolve over time, so must form documents. The project leader should be in regular contact with other attorneys to encourage comments on the forms. As discussed above, form documents should be stored (and viewable by users) in a DMS so that users may run blacklines to view changes that have been made to the forms over time. Clients expect that they are getting the "latest and greatest" language in their documents, and some of them may have an interest in understanding how and why standard language has changed over time. With blacklines and detailed annotations available to attorneys, there should be few client questions that junior associates lack the resources to address without senior attorney support.

Document automation

Document automation programs can be essential tools to support the drafting of documents for law firm clients under many circumstances. These platforms are often dismissed as being appropriate only if a firm is engaged in high-volume "commodity" drafting work, or if the firm is under pressure to deliver work at a lower cost or in connection with alternative fee arrangements; however, doing so could result in a missed opportunity.

Document automation programs should be considered whenever a firm finds that personnel are spending time engaged in mechanical drafting exercises. Any drafting that is done following a logical instruction can be done faster, cheaper, and better by a machine than by a human being. Though certainly most cost effective when applied to high volume work, using document automation technologies to draft highly complicated documents (and suites of related documents) not only makes the firm more competitive, but can produce better work than humans are capable of (thereby reducing risk to the firm and enhancing the firm's reputation).

The determinative factor is not the volume of work, but the volume of mechanical drafting – the volume of edits that human beings make that a machine could make. So, for example, if a 200-page securities offering prospectus form includes 1,000 mechanical edits, it should be a candidate for document automation, even if the document is prepared at a low volume.

Finally, an often-overlooked benefit of document automation programs is attorney satisfaction. Attorneys want to be engaged in interesting work. Indeed, attorney compensation is high because legal work generally requires the labor of highly educated individuals with excellent judgment and unique skills. To the extent that an attorney spends time engaged in mechanical drafting, the attorney is at risk of feeling underutilized and bored. Document automation programs can mitigate this risk.

How document automation programs work

Document automation programs generally operate by reading instructions that are embedded within word processing files, such as Microsoft Word files (programmed Word files are known as "templates"), to make mechanical edits to the document. The development process for a document automation project generally consists of three phases: first, establish the fields (also known as "variables") and calculations (collectively with variables known as "components") that will be used by the document template; second, embed the document template with code that links points within the template with the necessary variables and calculations; and third, develop the end user interface (or the "interview") that the attorneys will use to enter the data for a particular project.

When drafting a document based on a traditional form, the attorney starts at the beginning of the document and reads the drafting instructions, making edits as instructed. If a variable occurs more than once in a document (for example, the party names in an agreement will typically appear at least twice, in the preamble and the signature blocks), the drafter will need to make the edit multiple times. A document automation program, by comparison, makes all edits based on the established logic, which enables the platform to make several, if not hundreds, of edits based on a single variable. By using the technology to make all mechanical edits, the program can make thousands of edits in seconds that would have taken a human being hours.

Managing a document automation project

Document assembly projects are high-investment, high-risk projects for most law firms. Though the technology is relatively inexpensive, a substantial investment must be made to first develop the forms on which the automated templates will be based (see above), select the forms to be included in the platform, convert the forms into automated templates and build the user interview interface, and maintain the platform and the related templates and forms. At any point in this process, there is a high risk of failure if the project is not managed carefully.

Form selection

When determining whether to include a form in a document automation platform, several criteria must be evaluated, including the number of variables/components the form requires compared to the number of edits the program will make based on the variables/components, the level of custom drafting typically required, and the current workflow used to draft the document without a document automation program.

- **Ratio of variables/components to edits** – A document automation program is most valuable if the number of variables/components is a small fraction of the number of edits made based on those variables/components in the document or suite of documents. For example, if a template for a last will and testament includes 100 personal pronouns (e.g. his/her) that change depending on the gender of the testator, the user need only indicate once the gender of the testator and the program will make 100 edits, which could save the user about eight minutes of drafting time. This effect is magnified when applied across a suite of related forms and when a component is based on a sophisticated computation. Accordingly, if the ratio of variables/components to edits in a given document is one-to-one, the document might not be appropriate to add to a document automation platform.
- **Custom drafting** – Nearly all documents require some amount of custom drafting, but some require more than others. Of course, the greater the number of mechanical edits that a document automation

program can make to a document, the more appropriate the document is for the platform; and the greater the custom drafting, the less appropriate the document is for the platform.

- **Drafting workflow** – Some documents require only a single drafter, while others require several levels of review and comment from internal and external experts. Though a document automation interview may be designed with an electronic workflow built in so each expert fills in the relevant information at the time it is needed, building workflows around document automation platforms magnifies the complexity of the system and is rare in practice. Building a workflow may be appropriate and achievable for some firms, but extreme care must be taken when embarking on such a challenging project. More often, interviews are built so a single user enters the information in the interview. If the drafter typically does not have all (or most) of the information necessary to draft at the beginning of the drafting process, the program will often not be able to effectively assemble the document. Accordingly, for example, highly negotiated agreements are generally not suitable content for document automation platforms.

Technology selection

Once forms are finalized and determined as suitable for conversion into document automation templates, a document automation technology must be selected and deployed. Though a detailed description of how to select and deploy a technology solution for a law firm is beyond the scope of this chapter, it is worth noting that not all document automation technologies have the same capabilities (or price tags). When selecting the technology, the firm should understand, among other things, its requirements, the market penetration of the product, how long the product has been on the market, whether the product is that of an independent company or a subsidiary or division of a larger technology company, the experiences of current users of the product (functionality and support), to what extent third-party consultants will be required for deployment and maintenance of the platform, and the price. For reference, the commonly used document automation programs include Brightleaf, ContractExpress DealBuilder, Exari, and HotDocs. In addition, several practice management and other law firm technology products include document automation modules (for example, MatterSphere).

Designing variables/components, templates, and interviews

The process of designing variables and other components, templates, and interviews requires expertise in the document automation program's programming language and a deep understanding of the subject matter of the given form or suite of forms. This presents a challenge, as it is unusual for one person to have both of these skills. Document automation projects that outsource the entirety of the programming to third-party consultants have an increased risk that the structure of the data and the interview will not be consistent with user expectations. Furthermore, relying entirely on a consultant to build and maintain the platform may result in process bottlenecks and an over-reliance of the firm on a single consultant, which could lead to increased implementation and maintenance costs, among other negative consequences. However, it is equally unrealistic to expect an attorney, such as the project leader, to be able to become sufficiently knowledgeable in the programming language to design the platform on their own. Accordingly, the best approach to developing a document automation platform is for the bulk of the programming to be done internally by the project leader, with substantial training and support from consultants so that the system is built in a manner consistent with best practice.

Note that even after a form is added to a document automation platform, it may be appropriate to keep the form available to users outside of the platform, for example, in the DMS. Though assembly programs typically include a mechanism to view drafting instructions and annotations, some users may prefer viewing drafting instructions and annotations in the original form. Also, when proofreading the assembled document, users may need to compare the assembled document with the original form. For these reasons, the project leader may need to maintain duplicate versions of all forms, one as the document automation template, and the other as the original form.

Conclusion

As described above, there are many ways law firms prepare documents. The challenge for any law firm is to provide attorneys with the tools that enable them to prepare each document as efficiently as necessary to maintain the firm's competitive edge. The tools will vary by firm and by practice, but a firm that develops systems and processes that support the drafting of legal documents will have an advantage over one that does not, and in today's competitive legal services market, that could mean the difference between surviving and thriving.

Chapter 6:

Data-driven knowledge management – Matter lifecycle management

By Chad Ergun, director, global practice services and business intelligence at Gibson, Dunn & Crutcher LLP

We are living in an era of big data, promoted by low-cost storage and cloud computing, with the promise of advanced algorithms and increased adoption of internet of things (IoT). When combined with artificial intelligence, machine learning, and data visualization tools, these new solutions create the perfect breeding conditions for big data. Gartner defines "big data" as high-volume, high-velocity, and high-variety information assets that demand cost-effective, innovative forms of information processing for enhanced insight and decision making. Big data has yet another layer for advanced decision processing or decision support systems (DSS) called big data analytics. Big data analytics is the process of examining big data to uncover hidden patterns, unknown correlations, and other useful information that can be used to make better decisions. With big data analytics, data scientists and other specialists can analyze high volumes of data that conventional analytics or traditional business intelligence platforms cannot handle.

Big data is defined by the four dimensions of volume, velocity, variety, and value. These four Vs may be elaborated upon further as follows:

- **Volume:** Machine-generated data that is produced in much larger quantities than non-traditional data;
- **Velocity:** This refers to the speed of data processing, or the low latency rate at which analytics must be applied to the data, and looped back to the original sources of data to action;
- **Variety:** This refers to the large variety of input data (customer insights, competitive intelligence, trends, benchmarking data, standards, materials, etc.), which in turn generates a large variety of data as output; and

- **Value:** The economic value of different data varies significantly depending upon both the source and its end use. Firms must be clear at the outset about the business value big data initiatives will bring.

The rapid use of electronics and IT in products during the last two decades has resulted in many organizations sitting on an enormous amount of data – direct and indirect and/or past and present. Most IT systems used for product design, analysis, engineering, testing, and validation processes generate a large volume and variety of data. The increasing proliferation of computers and embedded electronics in the manufacturing industry, particularly in the automotive segment, has further resulted in the generation of a huge amount of structured and unstructured data. For example, use of computers and sensors in modern vehicles generates enormous data while a vehicle is in use.

The emerging challenge for organizations is to derive meaningful insights from available data and re-apply it intelligently. Knowledge management plays a crucial role in efficiently managing this data and delivering it to the end users to aid in the product development process. This involves collection of data from direct and indirect sources, analyzing and synthesizing it along with relevant enterprise data to derive meaningful information and intelligence, converting it into a useful knowledge base, storing it, and finally delivering it to end users.

To derive the maximum benefit from big data, organizations must modify their IT infrastructure to handle the rapid rate of delivery and extraction of huge volumes of data, with varying data types. These can then be integrated with the organization's enterprise data and analyzed. In fact, organizations, especially those with legacy systems, need to have a clear understanding of their past data and how the same can be merged into their current IT systems.

According to Yuan, Yoon, and Helendar, knowledge areas are classified into four types, collectively referred to as M-H-T-P: market knowledge, human knowledge, technology knowledge, and procedural knowledge. Based on these four knowledge areas, Table 1 depicts the mapping with elements of big data in the product development process.

Knowledge type	Volume	Velocity	Variety	Value
Market knowledge	• Customer data • Competitor data	• Direct interactions • Social media • Surveys	• Market analysis • Demographic data • Benchmarking data • Trends	• High value • Customer data • Competitor data
Human knowledge	• Experience based • Collaborative	• Real-time decision making	• Skill based • Experience based • Tacit knowledge	• Heuristic
Technology knowledge	• Standards • Usage • Materials • Field data	• Safety • Real-time data acquisition	• Cost • Reliability • Packaging • Ergonomics, etc.	• Patents
Procedural knowledge	• Design knowledge • Analysis • Materials std. • Verification, testing, and validation of knowledge	• Design knowledge • Std. materials library	• Design • CAD/CAM/CAE • Analysis • Manufacturing	• CAD/CAM/CAE data • Best practices • Test and validation • Service data • Manufacturing process data

Table 1: M-H-T-P

Knowledge management and big data

Big data has become so ubiquitous and integrated into our daily lives that it is expected to have significant effect on knowledge harvesting and sharing within an organization. The promised benefits of big data analytics combined with low cost, on-premises storage and cloud computing (lack of information governance notwithstanding), has created a data tsunami for many organizations. The first wave has hit e-discovery and resulted in significantly increased litigation and investigation costs. In response, e-discovery vendors have pushed back with advanced case analytics and case assessment tools in order to offer more predictability. The second wave is now about to revolutionize not only litigation or transactional practitioners, but overall matter lifecycle management, ranging from business intake to information governance and knowledge management.

Some of the early law firm adopters of big data analytics are adding chief data scientists (CDSs) to their KM teams and building data science teams to control the second wave of the data tsunami by using technology. Under the heavy pressure of technology advancements in data collection and processing, the conventional way of thinking about knowledge management for professional services is rapidly evolving.

Not long ago, the human element was a vital ingredient of big data analytics due to limitations within data science. We are now seeing impressive research results from MIT and technology vendors in replacing human intuition in pattern recognition by predicting and revealing those patterns. The same model applies to knowledge harvesting, collection, and distribution.

Some of the significant, but time consuming and costly, tasks of KM can be handled by big data analytics, pattern recognition algorithms, and machine learning systems. Instead of the push from professional support lawyers (PSLs) and resource attorneys, the new method could pull valuable data from different repositories using the technologies mentioned above to provide proactive solutions to fee earners and their clients. A well-designed strategy to support such a solution requires the ability to sense, acquire, transmit, process, store, and analyze the data to generate knowledge and distribute through different channels.

Law firm adoption

Law firms can utilize big data and KM in several areas: legal research, e-discovery, business intelligence, practice development, client sentiment analysis, budgeting, and financial planning.

1. **Learning from past practices:** A good place for firms to start is to make use of the historic data they already possess. Unfortunately, those are often in non-digitized form. Scanning old case documents, notes, and records can open a world of potential data that can be analyzed to give added depth to the firm's understanding of typical cases and practice matters.
2. **Client satisfaction rankings:** If a firm is trying to better understand clients' levels of satisfaction with the firm's services, email data is probably a good starting point. At the moment, email is the largest form of most unstructured firm data. Big data analytics can be used to survey things like client reactions, matter closing checklists, and billing-related issues. They can identify emotional responses to client communications, identifying words or phrases that negatively impact clients' acceptance of bills, or measure overall tone of the written communications.
3. **Speeding-up e-discovery:** Many e-discovery vendors tout the use of big data for improving overall experience and cost reduction.

Computer-assisted discovery is already the norm accepted by federal and state agencies. The addition of big data tools has the potential to make the process even more efficient. For example, it can increase the accuracy of predicting responsive documents and addressing investigation requests from government agencies. Some of these new tools can even be used for facial expression analysis that can then be utilized during mock trials to train litigators for the jury selection process. The same type of software has been used in the past with an audience watching the presidential debate to determine the "winner". McDonald's has also used it to determine how employees' moods affected the moods of its customers.

4. **Legal research:** The legal research and knowledge management tasks are excellent candidates for big data analytics. The true value of these analytics tools can be measured by introducing metrics to capture reactive and proactive legal research. Legal research fed by big data, internal KM repositories, and third-party content providers can easily provide a proactive platform to address fee-earners' needs before they ask for such information. A good example is a product called Ross, the world's first "digital attorney" powered by IBM Watson, which was developed by a group of students at the University of Toronto. Lawyers using Ross ask a legal question, and the program sifts through thousands of legal documents, statutes, and cases to provide an answer. Ross's responses include legal citations, suggest articles for further reading, and even calculate a confidence rating to help lawyers prepare for cases. Because Ross is a cognitive computing platform, it learns from past interactions, meaning that Ross's responses will grow to be more accurate as lawyers continue to use its system.

Matter lifecycle management

About six years ago, as a consultant, I was invited to attend a special committee meeting headed by a managing partner of a law firm to discuss practice technologies and major challenges facing fee earners. Surrounded by brilliant legal minds heading different practice areas, I asked if they could estimate average costs for different types of deals and engagements in various jurisdictions. I collected and shared their responses on-screen, showing three charts comparing the answers from practice heads, financial systems, and numbers based on my assessment. Needless to say, they were all different numbers. When I pitched the idea of technology-assisted matter budgeting, I was told by a transactional practice head that the process is hunch-based and does not require technology due to the complexity involved in calculating not only the direct cost but also in estimating potential risks and challenges.

Fast forward to 2015, and we are now dealing with a vast collection of data, armed with advanced technology, and working with millennials as fee earners. Due to the low cost of storage and need for data-driven decision systems, we are also hoarding data and storing transactional information. This new approach is making its way into our daily lives and is mostly observed as new technology in the consumer market. Major corporations, on the other hand, utilize the big data/advanced algorithms/artificial intelligence trio to cut costs, better understand human behavior, and make data-driven decisions. Examples range from parcel delivery companies tracking driver brake positions with GPS coordinates for better route management, to utilizing a large number of medical images for detecting diseases.

There are now specific applications riding this new wave of technology at law firms too. Some of them focus on e-discovery and litigation case management, and others target transactional practices. Using advanced case analytics and case assessment tools are becoming popular approaches for internal investigations and other e-discovery-related projects. Due to the highly complex nature of the legal process involved in litigation cases, cost predictability has become a major game changer. Unfortunately, costs for document review and e-discovery processes are adversely impacted by large volumes of content (another side-effect of data hoarding and cheap storage).

E-discovery technologies such as analytics for culling, early case assessment, and relevancy review are introducing major cost savings. Some companies are taking proactive measures and apply information governance (IG) to reduce data clutter, activate retention policies, and streamline content flow within their organizations. A well-established IG workflow significantly reduces the volume of documents and emails subject to discovery and review, providing substantial savings in both e-discovery costs and effort.

Similar technology and process re-engineering opportunities exist on the transactional side and are becoming more noteworthy. Fee earners working on corporate deals expect more predictive technology involvement in tracking their deals. They want automated notifications and better control over matter workflow. Other functions that can better utilize technology are deal budgeting, billing, and legal research.

Unlike the cost savings opportunities motivating litigators and clients for e-discovery, the initiatives focusing on transactional deals are more complicated to justify and show clear ROIs. When combined with lack of mainstream commercial products or supporting content, most of these initiatives cannot reach the production cycle for adoption by practicing attorneys.

So, how can we take advantage of big data, advanced technology, and information governance to address the needs of both transactional and litigation attorneys? The answer is a data-driven matter lifecycle management (MLM) platform with advanced algorithms and rich content harvested from big data initiatives. The concept behind MLM is very simple: track your deals and cases using advanced predictive technology and combine it with transactional data that used to be discarded. The concept of tracking matters from inception to closing is not new, and it does not require advanced technology, expensive tools, or major investment.

Pitch phase

MLM starts with the pitch phase as a pre-intake activity During this stage, pitches and proposals are put together based on past experience and similar deals, and are tailored to address clients' specific needs. Matter budgeting and staffing are other elements to consider at this point as well. In a fully populated MLM platform, the past experience, budget/cost analysis, profitability margins, fee-earner utilizations, and staffing analysis should be available to marketing staff and partners.

In addition to gathering data for a pitch or proposal, tracking the outcome of this phase is crucial and needs to be saved in the MLM platform. Authorized parties can search the collection and locate historical data about successful – or unsuccessful – proposals, better understand the clients' decision-making criteria, and build a trend analysis comparing the target to others in the same market and/or jurisdiction.

Relying on your CRM system and a collection of past pitches or proposals is no longer an industry best practice and does not provide competitive advantage over your competitors in the marketplace. Unfortunately, highly dynamic pricing models combined with shifting priorities and complex legal issues require an intelligent platform that updates itself based on each experience, activity, and response. Such an approach will help big law firms to introduce algorithmic marketing and provide more powerful solutions to partners, business development, and marketing staff.

Opening phase

After the completion of a successful pitch phase, a new matter and/or client intake phase starts based on the data gathered from the initial set of activities. The suggested best practice is to have a fully automated new business intake (NBI) workflow in place for this MLM phase.

The details captured can be included in the NBI to start the process, and are updated when the intake phase is complete. Relevant information can then be published on an internal intranet site for each client and matter. The opening phase integrates with other platforms such as finance, human resources, professional development, marketing, and training. Each end point for the NBI workflow can be monitored with automated notifications to ensure proper handling of new clients and matters. In addition to the audit trail created for compliance purposes, the same workflow can also provide KPIs to measure the time to open a new client/matter and detect any unusual delays in the process. These advanced processes built into the NBI workflow will reduce delays, and increase efficiency and utilization. The matters that are subject to confidentiality can be tagged at this phase and only made visible to the timekeepers of the matter team.

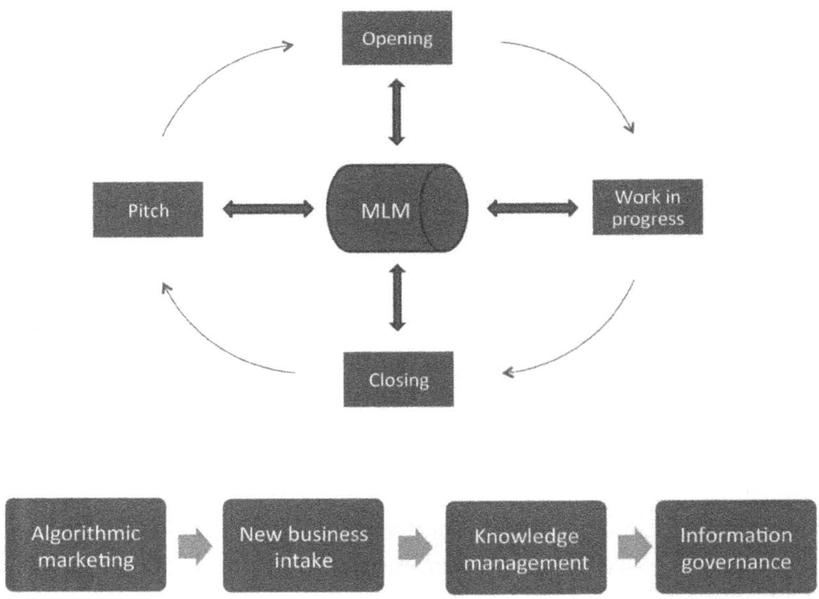

Figure 1: Matter lifecycle management workflow

Work in progress

The third step of MLM is the work in progress (WIP) phase. At this stage, proper client/matter numbers are already assigned, all conflict checks are completed, and related documentation such as engagement letters and billing guidelines are uploaded into the system. All activities in this phase can be pushed to the MLM platform for each matter and published on their intranet sites with appropriate security. It is here where KM plays a major role in helping attorneys locate actionable content, model documents, and precedents. Some of the most visible practice technologies such as knowledge libraries, enterprise search, predictive coding, legal project management, research, and other KM solutions are used by fee earners.

An algorithm-based proactive decision workflow can be used to direct attorneys and their support staff to a correct set of resources and improve legal research activities. Some of the other approaches include sharing matter updates and relevant documents with clients by utilizing automated notifications. You can also take advantage of big data, news feeds, and social media updates to trigger alerts to notify all parties involved in specific deals. Any unusual activity can be monitored to prevent unauthorized content modification, access, and other audit elements.

Closing

The last phase of MLM is the matter closing. This stage can be triggered by pre-set threshold variables such as number of hours billed, uploading deal closing sets, or direct updates from the partner in charge of the matter. The system can initiate automated matter closing notifications to alert authorized parties and obtain final approval to star the matter closing tasks. Once the closing is finalized, the retention cycle based on IG rules is initiated. Depending on variables included in the deal profiles, certain matters can be released to internal resources. The closing phase also involves the records department as the last stop for executed documents for recordkeeping purposes.

After a successful implementation of MLM with advanced analytics, you should be able to:

- Search deals based on location, industry, or closing value and combine that with attorney expertise and availability to build matter teams;

- Create matter budgets within 5–10 percent accuracy range;
- Locate valuable KM content such as precedents based on deal profile search;
- Receive alerts when an unusual activity is detected within the MLM workflow;
- Get daily summary updates about active matters and content shared with clients and other third parties; and
- Set up custom alerts to monitor major milestones.

The value of MLM

Matter lifecycle management processes can enable law firms to fully integrate predictive technologies that streamline client-matter workflow, resource management, budgeting, and legal project management. But a mature MLM will require well-designed new business intake (NBI), information governance (IG), and actionable content. Without these pillars to support the process, MLM will fail in the long term.

On the technology side, MLM needs to offer a proactive approach with advanced features and intelligent workflow to get fee earners engaged. For example, receiving alerts while drafting a credit agreement that precedents or similar content already exists in your KM library. Actionable intelligence combined with behavioral analytics will bring significant value to MLM and will improve the overall user experience.

Historically, law firms are not early adopters of advanced technology due to a potentially high risk-to-benefit ratio and lack of R&D resources, but we are now facing unprecedented force and velocity of disruptive technologies. These new solutions (such as Watson-like artificial intelligence tools, predictive coding, decision-making algorithms, big data with visualization, and cloud-based SaaS), combined with cost-cutting efforts resulting from the financial crisis, are early indications of a new era. Believe it or not, the legal industry is in the midst of an analytics revolution. Some of the early adopters are building data science teams and are hiring chief data scientists (CDS) to control the explosion of big data by using technology. Others are already using these technologies on a daily basis during case review and early case assessment, or for document review with predictive coding.

Currently, hunch and gut-feelings are the dominant decision-making methods in the corporate world. If you are in a volatile market facing rapidly changing variables, relying on judgment calls based on past experience is becoming increasingly unreliable. However, exclusively depending on big data analytics and science will block your long-term vision and force you to make reactive and short-term decisions. Therefore, you need a decision-making approach that combines the key elements of data analytics with past management experience. This is where MLM plays a major role, offering lawyers, business development, and marketing staff a new way to profile, track, and search deals. Most importantly, it offers them a new way to make data-driven decisions.

Chapter 7:
Blockchain technology can inform the legal profession

By Michael Dov Nogroski, director of practice innovations at Chapman and Cutler LLP

It is a difficult task in early 2016 to sort through the massive amount of literature on blockchain technology. There is incredible enthusiasm and the buzz seems to be at an all-time high. Many proponents who see a better future through the spread of this technology claim that this is a true game-changer, something that will transform finance, businesses, and the world in the same way that the internet has driven tremendous change in the last 20 years.

Predictions in this blockchain area are difficult to endorse. Although it has been several years since the dawning of this technology, this is still a very new phenomenon and real world applications are extremely limited and lack maturity. Perhaps the blockchain phenomenon has hit its peak of interest, principally in the promise and propaganda of what is to come, while naysayers and critics emerge more widely to warn that this all will pass without any net change or real-world adoption of this technology. The momentum indicates that there's more on the horizon.

Notwithstanding some of the criticism and doubt that has been voiced, there seems to be significant positive interest in this technology. Investment continues to roll in to start-ups and newly formed companies developing blockchain applications and products. Companies such as Digital Asset, Ripple, Ethereum, and Hedgy are just a few examples. They have names that sound appropriate for technology start-ups, but more importantly they are forging ahead to create solutions that have real world utility. They are exploring ways for banks to connect directly to each other, without intermediaries, in transactions such as cross-border payments. They are working to speed up transactions and solve problems of settlement latency. They are developing frameworks to track assets (diamonds, in one interesting example, for start-up Everledger) using unique identifiers, and via the blockchain framework these assets are tracked and traceable so they can later be leveraged for other digital trading or transactions. Digital Asset was even recently selected by the Australian Securities Exchange to develop solutions for the Australian market, with a focus on improving post-trade processing, tying in to plans the exchange already had to work on replacing its current platform.

The largest banks in the world are hiring developers and consultants to work on this technology. They are also acquiring or partnering with many of the smaller start-ups already developing blockchain technology. Some banks are now filing patents for specific use cases. The venture capital world has also taken an active interest with high-profile firms such as Andreesen Horowitz and Kleiner Perkins Caufield & Byers adding their names to the list of those investing. And then there are other players investing as well, including IBM, Visa, Nasdaq, Samsung, to name a few. These examples represent a small fraction of the attention and focus that the technology is earning. Even beyond these organizations that have been directly investing, other organizations such as the Big Four accounting firms are also starting to get more involved and to claim their public relations stake, putting it out that they are interested in and recognize the importance of this emerging technology.

Blockchain – A basic explanation

For those not following this development or who are unfamiliar with it, what is the blockchain? It is commonly explained as a decentralized electronic general ledger. Basically, it is a framework to facilitate and record transactions on a distributed network comprising thousands (perhaps more, or less) of different nodes. Every single transaction is recorded in the ledger and a network of computers works to enforce controls that validate transactions in a method that is purportedly fraud-proof and trustworthy via protections of the entire network and within the cryptographic features and digital signature verification methods. All the transactions are stored or recorded in blocks, and all the transactions are chained together, hence the name. It is the underlying technology on which Bitcoin, the digital cryptocurrency that has gained prominent attention in the news, runs.

A more detailed description of blockchain mechanics warrants more focus than a few paragraphs in an article, and this article does not seek to describe entirely how the blockchain works. There are numerous explanations available in countless other articles and materials. More importantly, developing an accurate and meaningful understanding of the technology is not something that is simple to undertake.

The blockchain concept garners much attention as a conduit for exchanging money through its platform, but there are two very important and promising considerations for blockchain technology's future as this technology moves out of the shadow of Bitcoin and gains attention on its own account. First, the blockchain can serve as an architectural advancement in database structure and efficacy. Second, the development of applications leveraging blockchain technology can serve to facilitate simple or sophisticated agreements between parties where these "agreements" can run automatically without human interaction or interference. Both of these considerations can have an impact on knowledge management concepts and legal practice.

A new database

Some herald the blockchain as representing a paradigm shift in software design, serving in the role of a new type of database. Effectively, this is the decentralized ledger. As a "ledger" a system can capture details such as timestamps and unique identifiers for information, or in the Internet of Things (IoT) it could map to RFID tags on physical assets. The stored information can then potentially be leveraged for other transactions, trading, or for verification and tracking purposes. The details are recorded and the information is appended and replicated across the entire network. Every node gets the latest update in information.

As the blockchain adds records, they are chained together. All previous transactions are stored and there is a kind of immutable integrity as the prior transactions cannot be manipulated or removed. Through this decentralization and ability to arrive at verifiable authoritative information on the blockchain network, intermediaries ostensibly are not needed and transactions can move more quickly. Slow back-office operations are avoided, as are standstill periods where a transaction is on hold until an individual can get to a task or until a queue is cleared, and blockchains can even be programmed to conform to regulatory requirements.

The technology is currently being contemplated for a vast variety of purposes. Discussions are being conducted with governments to consider storing an assortment of records such as licenses, certificates, titles, and documents. The idea of "smart cities" that digitally track and record information via sensors and other systems could employ blockchain technology to store the information and correspondingly track city assets. Activity and data trends could be captured and then inform the system to automatically respond when certain scenarios arise, with specific actions based on the nature and availability of city assets. As one example, if crime patterns arise in certain areas of a city, police patrols could be redeployed to those areas automatically. As another example, water distribution could be increased or rerouted based on weather patterns. There are myriad ways in which applications could arise, and whereas many of the ideas of the IoT or "smart cities" do not rely on blockchain technology, proponents have offered that the blockchain design offers up greater authoritative veracity.

As a platform for "smart contracts"

Optimists and enthusiasts are also suggesting that blockchain technology could be used for many transactions, even non-financial agreements, serving as a next-level program for agreements in the form of "smart contracts". These are self-automated programs that will carry out the terms of a contract via the network. Some predict the growth of blockchain as a future platform for deals and transactions that will do things like automatically initiate payment when performance is met. A simple example is a payment automatically sent or released upon another system or data feed updating to indicate the completed delivery of goods.

Fundamentally, smart contracts are computer applications implemented via computer code. The blockchain technology provides the verification pieces and will allow for actions to be updated as new transactions once information is supplied to indicate that a condition or obligation has been met. By their very nature, employing code and primarily if-then statements, there is no room for vagueness or ambiguity. The program must know how to determine when a condition is met. The actions to take must be clear enough for a computer to handle. Once in place, humans (attorneys included) are not needed. Other third parties such as credit card processors or banks can be avoided as well.

It is also possible, although less popularized, that there may be hybrid approaches. This could apply to a combination of smart contracts and not-so-smart contracts (on paper) where the more straightforward and absolute contractual aspects get codified in the program, but the less absolute aspects such as language that refers to "reasonable" standards, gets memorialized in a corresponding paper or hard-copy contract. Another hybrid approach may be to have actions automated via the smart contract that are part of an overall workflow involving some human interaction. This could very well involve elements of business process management and notification workflow. A smart contract runs on its own, but if there are specific triggers invoked, the system could automatically notify designated personnel to review. This is much less appealing to advocates who maintain that computers can handle all the work, but contracting parties may want the benefit of automation with built-in controls to avoid immediate actions if some obligations are not fulfilled or if there is some interpretation to be provided.

Knowledge management

The ideas materializing and being converted into startup attempts that leverage blockchain technology serve to answer some interesting knowledge management challenges that have existed for some time. First, there is information that can be made accessible on the network. The information on a blockchain platform won't supply the tacit knowledge that companies and knowledge management proponents attempt to capture through collaboration and contribution to portals, intranets, and knowledge communities. It is far more mundane as explicit knowledge. It is as boring as a ledger sounds, a series of information recordings coded as if they were bar codes waiting to be scanned. However, the utility exists in the potential to keep permanent records that are not centralized or trapped behind a single firewall. They can be made available as a decentralized ledger that can be accessed and relied on for accuracy. These records can then connect to other systems, providing responsive data to affect other data or workflows.

The rise of smart contracts can further respond to knowledge management challenges, combining both explicit and tacit knowledge by way of developing contract building blocks that could be leveraged for various contracts. Much in the same way that many lawyers and practice groups within a law firm attempt to establish form documents or more granular clause libraries (often to limited effect), given the complexity of computer code there will be a heightened focus on modularity and an effort to contemplate contracts more as building blocks that can be re-used as needed. Over time, contract and provision libraries will be more widely available and there may be code/library distributions that are lauded for their excellence.

Legal issues and other challenges

If smart contracts on the blockchain are to take off, there are numerous ways in which this might relate to the legal world, and it also raises legal questions. For many individuals and entities as parties to a deal or an agreement, it is difficult to understand all the contractual legal terms and provisions even when written in plain (or not-so-plain) English. Some details may be more complex and involve highly intricate language that serves to deal with unique circumstances, meet regulations, or avoid loss if any form of dispute resolution were to ensue in the future. Lawyers often enter the picture to assist, particularly when the assets in play are significant, or the stakes involved are high. Parties seek protection or, in other instances, bear risks that need to be carefully set forth and documented because future events and conditions, met or unmet, trigger actions and implications.

Parties leveraging a blockchain platform to conduct a transaction or carry out a deal will require assurance that the underlying code to facilitate a deal maps to their understanding of what they are committing to in terms of their obligations. When agreements are reduced to code, many parties and even their lawyers are ill equipped to understand and thoroughly validate the agreement terms. They may have to rely on a programmer's explanation of the code. Conversely, a programmer must have sufficient understanding of the legal and contractual requirements to properly represent the rights of the parties. This is all the more critical when working with an electronic platform that can automatically initiate actions as defined in the "contract" on a blockchain platform. Like sophisticated software shops, it will require testing and quality control prior to deployment. It is not typical to find hybrid lawyer/coders, although there is a burgeoning community, and in the future, with the efforts of institutions like Stanford and their Center for Legal Informatics (CodeX), there may be a rise in a new type of lawyer.

More questions and issues abound as one starts to reflect on the challenges and potential risks that could arise in a networked system that automatically invokes actions based on conditional criteria. For one thing, if certain parties and their lawyers do not sufficiently understand the underlying code, can some parties gain an unfair advantage? Will enforceability become a prominent issue even though these systems are supposed to enforce themselves? What will happen when parties seek recourse and redress through the courts? And if a complaint makes it to court, how will courts review agreements on a blockchain or similar platform if they are not capable of reading the agreement and terms in the same way that they would currently review a contract drafted in Microsoft Word?

In addition, there are potential scenarios that could spark inquiry from regulators. This is already starting to take place and Bitcoin has come under some review and scrutiny. Some supporters of these technologies are engaged and energized by the very idea that third-party regulators are not required here, in a platform that subscribes to a system of distributed autonomous organization. However, if government agencies start to knock on the door, as they have started to do, what happens next? It could cast a cloud over the efforts and slow expert contributions from the community that supports a system free from intermediaries.

There are potential ways to mitigate legal concerns with blockchain technology and approach the future with greater confidence. One is for those who work in the legal industry to gain a deeper understanding of blockchain and what it portends. This can be accomplished by learning more about coding concepts, information delivery, and security protocols. If there are more knowledgeable authors of smart contracts, whether coding directly or capably working with development teams, that will help to ensure validity of the legal constructs utilized within. Another approach is to more deeply embrace knowledge management concepts and make use of established platforms that have trusted and valued code built in so that they can be leveraged for various agreements. Some newer platform solutions may arise that seek to mitigate the coding obfuscation by virtue of a higher level language that reads more like English text but effectively translates to more sophisticated code to carry out its functions.

A lot is still unknown at this point. Whether blockchain technology truly takes off remains to be seen. It may take years before things start to take shape. Nevertheless, it is important for lawyers to remain apprised of developments like these. Advancements in contract drafting and overall transaction workflow will eventually come to fruition. Those attorneys who can navigate through the more intricate aspects of technology will have an advantage over those who do not. Moreover, they will be better positioned to represent their clients in a world that increasingly demands technology expertise. Alternatively, they may be well positioned to shift into new roles if computers do in fact take over some of the work. Whether it is the ability to code smart contracts, understand how data is stored in databases and moves across a network, or work with various algorithms to train systems, detect patterns, or establish secure hash functions, these skills will matter as everything becomes more connected.

Part Two
Case studies

Case study 1:
Innovation as a business development strategy

By Scott Rechtschaffen, chief knowledge officer, and James Durham, chief marketing and business development officer, at Littler Mendelson

Law firm marketing approaches have evolved

Consider the marketing phrases that law firms have gone through in an effort to differentiate themselves from their competition. Once, law firm collateral, websites, and advertising focused on "great lawyering" – essentially, saying our attorneys are smarter and more skilled than the attorneys at the other firms. Then, law firm marketing shifted to a focus on "partnering" and "collaborating" with clients – claiming their attorneys understood clients' business better than the attorneys at other firms. More recently, it seems to be about being "cost effective".

But, how exactly does a firm – say a firm ranked as number 76 on the AmLaw 100 list – demonstrate through its website or advertising copy that its attorneys are smarter, or that they are better client partners than, say, the attorneys at a firm ranked as AmLaw number 39, 79, or 86? With bios showing where its attorneys went to law school? With lists or anonymized case studies? Can law firms seriously market their advantage over competitors with claims of greater intellectual prowess or saying they are more cost effective? Saying so does not necessarily make these firms better value. Are these really the attributes that distinguish one law firm from another? Firms highlight their attorneys' knowledge of a client's business and its industry. It is impossible to be a great lawyer without that, but it's not a differentiator – it's table stakes.

In the past few years, many law firms have begun to focus their marketing and brand-building efforts on a tangible attribute to significantly differentiate themselves from the competition using "innovation". However, true "innovation" is more than a passing buzzword, or the marketing phrase of the moment. It is a strategy for improving the delivery of legal services and positively impacting the law firm-client relationship to the benefit of both. Innovation strategies include developing robust knowledge management programs, providing clients with comprehensive legal information offerings, implementing legal process management and legal process improvement methodologies, and deploying genuinely cutting-edge technology (i.e. beyond iPhone and Android apps, sophisticated websites, and extranets).

Why innovation is relevant for today's corporate legal clients

Developing an innovation strategy is much more than a marketing device because innovation, used this way, addresses the most critical demands that corporate legal clients are now making of their outside counsel. Since the Great Recession of 2008 and its impact on the legal industry, clients have increasingly demanded a change in the way their law firms deliver services. For most firms, the days of routine annual rate increases and ill-defined – or "blank check" – budgets for legal matters are a distant memory from the golden days of the legal industry. Now, clients demand reduced costs, increased efficiency, greater transparency, and higher quality standards. In-house counsel have greater leverage than ever to change the way their outside counsel deliver legal services. Corporate clients also have more options to get the legal resources they need. What many attorneys and law firms do not realize is that they are no longer just competing with other law firms; they are competing with Google and the vast array of resources that the web offers.

Today, an innovation strategy has to be much more than the technology "innovations" that law firms have adopted over the past decades – email, smartphones, online legal research, extranets, and e-filing. These have been sustainable innovations enabling lawyers to communicate and collaborate with their clients more efficiently, but they did not fundamentally change how legal services were delivered and by whom. The newly emerging technologies – for example, predictive coding, document automation, and "expert advisor" systems, such as Littler's ComplianceHR suite of products, discussed below – are disruptive technologies. Over time, they will vastly reduce the need for, respectively: attorney-performed document review; attorneys drafting routine documents; and attorneys answering basic client questions.

Legal services have largely remained a one-attorney-to-one-user interaction model (or a many-attorney-to-one-client model). But the rest of the world leverages technology on a one-provider-to-hundreds-or-thousands-of-users model. It is unreasonable to believe that lawyers will remain a unique coterie of professionals delivering bespoke services, while the rest of the world – including every other major profession – has moved further into the online mainstream. As legal industry prognosticator Richard Susskind has noted: "It is simply inconceivable that information technology will radically alter all corners of our economy and society and yet somehow legal work will be exempt from any change."[1]

For innovation to become more than just a marketing phrase, for a law firm to truly establish its brand as an "innovative" law firm, it must develop and implement a strategy that truly transforms how legal services – legal information, litigation, advice and counseling, transactional work – are delivered. It is insufficient to simply "check the box" by launching one or two apps or adding more generic articles and news alerts to a firm's website. A true innovation strategy envisions dramatically and comprehensively changing the way firms interact with and serve their clients that helps clients make money, save money, look good, or sleep better. A successful innovation strategy cannot just change the game, it has to change it for the better.

Innovation at Littler

At Littler, we have spent the past two decades developing and implementing just such an innovation strategy. We began by offering clients a robust knowledge management program, with a content marketing strategy that delivered critical, valuable legal, business, and legislative insights in a way that other firms could seldom match. More recently, though, we have moved to develop technology tools, legal processes, and products that offer our clients alternatives to the traditional one-to-one client-attorney relationship and the billable hour model.

Through these efforts, Littler has become widely recognized as an innovative law firm – it has become a core component of our brand, if you will. Over the past few years we have been consistently recognized by major publications, and both the firm and our individual attorneys have received awards for innovation. Increasingly, we are hearing clients reference our investment in innovative service solutions as a differentiator.

The beginnings of innovation at Littler – Knowledge management

About 15 years ago, a number of major US law firms began adding knowledge management functions to their corporate infrastructure. Many hired chief knowledge officers or directors of knowledge management. Initially, the goal was to enhance access to the treasure trove of precedential work product that law firms seemingly generate in their sleep – model transactional documents, best practice forms and policies, pleadings and litigation documents, and advice memos. In those early days, knowledge management was designed to prevent lawyers from constantly re-inventing the wheel by providing them with access to the best work product already created by experienced colleagues within their firms. This would, of course, increase efficiency and save clients time and money.

Naturally, many firms turned to technology solutions. Often, knowledge management became an adjunct to the IT department and the leading advocates for knowledge management were those law firm partners who had a real passion for and fascination with technology. Firms developed and deployed expertise databases, enterprise search systems, and elaborate subject-matter intranets. Similarly, at Littler, our knowledge management program focused initially on providing the firm's attorneys with ready access to the enormous amount of precedential work product, and it eased access to the firm's subject matter experts. We developed internal databases and collections of substantive materials. We deployed an enterprise search platform that enabled attorneys to quickly find the work product they needed to work more efficiently and avoid re-creating the wheel in serving their clients.

However, Littler realized that focusing knowledge management solely on improving internal attorney efficiency ignored the advantages that a robust knowledge management program could contribute to the firm's service to its clients, as well as the firm's brand and overall marketing efforts.

Knowledge management as the foundation of a comprehensive content marketing strategy

Recognizing the brand value and importance of truly leveraging firm-created content, Littler's knowledge management program began to focus extensively on creating and aggregating valuable substantive content in ways that informed clients of critical developments and demonstrated the firm's deep and broad subject matter expertise. This was a natural evolution of Littler's already heavy investment in content dissemination that demonstrated its substantive legal knowledge and analysis. Littler first published *The National Employer®* book before it had a single office outside of California – which naturally helped develop Littler's brand as a national law firm even before we were truly national in geographic scope. Similarly, Littler published its *Guide to International Employment and Labor Law* before it had a single office outside of the United States – again, helping to develop Littler's global brand before we had a presence in 14 countries, as we do today. In both instances, the smart development and distribution of content helped define Littler's brand, providing a natural base for our knowledge and expertise.

Initially, these knowledge management efforts included not only client conferences, client alerts, and newsletters, but also comprehensive compendiums with in-depth analysis of pertinent legal issues and developments. Some of these publications and content initiatives are:

- **The *Employer Series* publications:** Littler developed this print publication series over 30 years ago to be a comprehensive primer of employment and labor law. Initially, the *The National Employer®* book was created as a loose-leaf notebook designed to be handed out at client conferences. Over time, Littler developed relationships with major legal content publishers to transform that thin notebook into an exhaustive 6,000-plus page encyclopedia covering federal law and the law of over 30 states – published in both print and digitally. Today, it ranks as one of the most comprehensive compendiums of US employment and labor law.
- **Legal developments alerts:** Littler typically publishes about 250 legal development alerts each year in various formats – as electronic newsletters, client alerts, and blog posts. These are sent directly to clients, posted on the firm's website, posted to social media sites, and distributed through various channels such as Mondaq, Lexology, JD Supra, and others. At one point, Littler maintained 11 separate blogs covering topics as diverse as workplace privacy, global employment law developments, global immigration, electronic discovery, and wage-hour law. (Littler's blogs have since been incorporated into Littler's overall content platform and no longer exist as traditional stand-alone blogs.)
- **White papers and Littler reports:** Every year, Littler publishes in-depth white papers and reports covering major developments and coming trends in employment and labor law. Littler's *Annual Report on EEOC Developments* has been published annually for the past five years and provides a comprehensive examination of significant events and enforcement activities of the Equal Employment Opportunity Commission. Published in 2012, Littler's *"Bring Your Own Device" to Work Movement* report, co-authored by over 20 Littler attorneys, was a pioneering examination of the growing BYOD trend and its potential impact on employment law in the workplace. This Littler report helped

enhance the reputation of Littler's burgeoning workplace privacy and data security practice group.

- **Single-subject publications:** Littler has also worked with many of the major legal industry publishers on books dedicated to specific topics within the field of employment and labor law. Our attorneys have developed authoritative publications that enable us to say, truly, that "we wrote the book" on major subject areas of interest to our clients.[2]

Recently, the CEO of one of the leading online legal research platforms observed that, with its prolific output, Littler must surely rank as one of the top 10 leading producers of legal content in the US. He then asked how Littler was able to generate such a huge volume of content given that most attorneys are generally incentivized and compensated for generating client work, not writing books and white papers.

How do we do it?

There are really several answers to this question. First, with its long history of using content to market the firm's authoritative knowledge and expertise in the field of employment and labor law, it had become part of our firm culture that attorneys were expected to contribute to the firm's publishing efforts. Second, Littler has always stressed the importance of individual attorneys becoming "subject matters experts" in the many sub-domains that make up the field of employment and labor law. Attorneys who wish to develop business and new clients – and get referrals of business from within the firm – were encouraged to establish themselves in fields that were critical to our clients, such as privacy, employee benefits, executive compensation, and union-management relations. Writing and publishing on those topics is one of the best ways to do so.

Clearly, Littler's investment in building a substantial knowledge management (KM) department is one of its significant advantages and critical resources. Our KM department was established in 2001. Currently, Littler has over 15 dedicated knowledge management counsel (all attorneys with significant employment and labor experience). We have three dedicated research attorneys and over 15 professionals on our research and library team. All work together to generate a large amount of legal content that is valuable to our clients.

Within this larger group, we have a dedicated content publishing team that is responsible for producing initial drafts, reviewing content with attorney subject-matter experts, editing the content received from SMEs, and preparing and formatting content for publication. To ensure quality, most content generated by Littler attorneys is reviewed prior to publication by our publications review committee – a group consisting of knowledge management counsel and over 50 attorneys from across the firm, representing most of our major practice areas.

In addition to Littler's knowledge management department, the firm's client relations and marketing (CR&M) department plays an equally critical role in Littler's content marketing strategy. The CR&M team oversees the distribution of Littler's content through its numerous online channels, and manages the many content distribution relationships Littler maintains with third parties, whether they be subscribers or syndicators, and increasingly we are using data analytics to refine our content distribution strategies. The CR&M team is further leveraging Littler's content through an increasingly more robust social media and public relations strategy that takes full advantage of the brand-building opportunities social media provides.

Innovative legal service solutions as a brand differentiator for Littler

While a comprehensive content marketing program that provides clients and prospective clients with critical legal information plays an important role in a firm's innovation strategy, it is only one prong of a broader strategy. The firm must also demonstrate by its actions – as well as in its marketing – that it is committed to innovation, by being willing to change the way clients and lawyers work together.

About 10 years ago, Littler began taking its KM strategy to the next level. Using many of the same teams and enhanced content, we began building online tools – "service solutions" – that would give clients direct access to the firm's knowledge management and other useful resources. Our first major effort was Littler GPS®, an online subscription service that provided clients with access to a comprehensive database of multi-jurisdiction surveys – covering topics as diverse as minimum wage requirements or lactation accommodation obligations across every major US jurisdiction. Because employment law requirements are often state-specific, employers need to be aware of the various requirements across the jurisdictions in which they operate. Eventually, Littler GPS grew to cover over 65 employment law topics and included weekly updates of new legislative and regulatory developments in any jurisdiction.

Next, we began to provide online toolkits providing clients with access to information and resources covering specific industries and subject areas. For example, our Home Care Toolkit provides online compliance resources for employers in the home health care industry. Our Littler X-celerator™ provides start-up companies with access to resources to help them keep their growing businesses compliant with federal and California employment laws. Littler HR PolicySmart™ is an online resource enabling any company to keep track of changes in legal requirements that might impact their HR policies and procedures.

More recently, Littler launched two of its most ambitious offerings: Littler CaseSmart® and ComplianceHR. Littler CaseSmart represents, in our view, the future of employment law. It is a completely re-imagined process for managing administrative charges, single-plaintiff litigation, and employment law class actions. It combines proprietary technology, an alternative staffing model, and a completely differentiated workflow process for handling legal matters. In the past five years we have handled over 12,000 administrative charges and almost 400 litigation matters using this process, providing our clients with significant cost savings as well as transparent access to matter management.

ComplianceHR is a unique joint venture between Littler and Neota Logic, a leading legal technology software provider. ComplianceHR's suite of products enable in-house counsel to efficiently handle routine requests from their internal HR and business unit clients, answering important but repetitive questions such as whether a given employee qualifies as overtime exempt or whether an individual can lawfully be engaged as an independent contractor. ComplianceHR also offers applications that generate routine documents such as employment agreements, NDAs, and non-competes.

Conclusion

These various initiatives represent Littler's effort to provide unique and innovative services to its clients, recognizing that many legal services will inevitably move to an online service delivery model; not overnight, but over time. We are attempting to emulate, and move with clients to, the web-based service delivery model that is now the norm in virtually every other industry.

Of course, we recognize that there will always be a need for a trusted advisor – lawyers who can work with clients to develop bespoke strategies and solutions, delivering premium advice and counseling. So while we know that there are limits to the services that can be delivered to clients online, we strongly believe that being at the forefront of developing unique legal services in ways that can help our clients be more successful demonstrates a genuine commitment to client service. It is also a reflection of our commitment to making innovation a key part of our brand.

References

1. Susskind, R., *Tomorrow's Lawyers: An Introduction to Your Future*, Oxford University Press, 2013.

2. These publications currently include, among others: *Littler Mendelson on Employment Law Class Actions* (LexisNexis, Third Edition); *Whistleblowing & Retaliation* (LexisNexis, 5th edition); *The Littler Mendelson Guide to International Employment & Labor Law* (LexisNexis, 4th edition); *Disability Discrimination and the Workplace* (BNA, 2nd edition); *Unfair Competition and Intellectual Property Protection in Employment Law: Contract Solutions and Litigation Guide* (BNA); *Wage and Hour Answer Book* (Wolters Kluwer Law & Business).

Case study 2: Changing the way knowledge is used to support clients

Fiona Parkinson, head of knowledge management at BLM

BLM is the leading risk and insurance law specialist in the UK. We aim to be recognized as one globally by 2020. We are proud of our established and deep-rooted presence in the general insurance sector, the Lloyd's and London Market, and amongst brokers. We also have a significant presence amongst corporate clients, in the public sector, and in the health and care industry. BLM also has an existing strong remit of international work and contacts, representing UK companies operating abroad, acting for a breadth of international organizations, and handling high-profile multijurisdictional cases.

2014–15 was a year of great evolution and growth for BLM and, with more than 200 partners and over 800 legal experts, it has become increasingly essential for internal knowledge management practices to evolve. We know how important it is to use all of our skills, training, and intelligence to make our clients' lives better and to make our clients more successful, and the role of knowledge management in this process is fundamental. The firm prides itself on providing clients with solutions that are clear and concise, delivering a service that is consistent and reliable, and building connected relationships that are strong and enduring. A powerful thought leadership and knowledge management (KM) capability to maximize the firm's expertise is therefore key to our business and our ability to compete.

BLM is looking to change the way it identifies, collects, and uses knowledge and content to engage and support clients. The business has grown by 50 percent in the last five years and we now have 13 offices in the UK and Ireland. We must ensure we are aware of the knowledge we have internally and who owns that knowledge. With that in mind, I was appointed to develop the firm's KM strategy, to surface, manage, and use the combined knowledge of our employees for the good of our business and our relationships with clients. Formalizing the KM function across the firm is a step-change in our approach and it is exciting to be at the forefront of this.

The starting point

The most important starting point for me was to understand what clients expect from BLM and what the firm is looking to achieve. My first step was to get to know the firm's developing strategy, and to speak to the sector and business stream heads to understand what they were looking to achieve, as well as their pain points. This insight helped me to develop a firm-wide KM strategy in the form of a one page summary that, crucially, could be shared and understood by everyone. The strategy articulates what KM means to BLM, the benefits a streamlined KM function will bring to the firm, and the plan for the first few months to deliver benefits. All of which is aligned with the firm's objectives. Essential to the success of the strategy, and the KM function overall, is support from the top, which allows us to address any barriers and to move things forward.

Overall governance is very important. At BLM, our KM strategy group includes senior representatives from learning and development, HR, IT, and knowledge management to steer and deliver the strategy approved by our executive board.

We have looked at the strategy in terms of people, processes, and technology. While knowledge management is everyone's responsibility and everyone needs to be involved to make it a success, we need coordinators, KM professionals, or (as they are known in the UK) professional support lawyers (PSLs) in place representing each practice group to create and identify important know-how. They make sure this is managed and shared appropriately across the firm, researching, writing content, categorizing, storing, and training. They may also take their know-how to client relationship meetings, ensuring they are kept up to date on anything that might affect them, or that they would benefit from knowing about. KM professionals are key to ensuring knowledge hidden in emails, network folders, within matters, and in people's heads is captured and shared.

People

With this in mind, I have started to build on our existing PSL role, standardizing it across the firm and promoting its importance. I have developed a new PSL job description, making sure this is seen as a parallel career to the fee-earning lawyer. Part of this work has been talking to business stream heads to ensure we have PSL coverage across the organization and we are currently recruiting to fill in the gaps. PSLs will report in to their own specialist business areas as well as being integrated into a wider KM

Group, including information services, marketing and communications, business development, and learning and development. This facilitates fully joined-up processes to research, create, and manage information, and to surface it for re-use externally and internally.

PSLs are described as "the lawyer's lawyer" in the industry, and our existing PSLs are seen as invaluable time-savers to lawyers who have to meet tight deadlines and the demands of sophisticated clients. Being able to advise a client on a discrete but complex legal issue and having the satisfaction that it has been well-researched is really important in a fiercely competitive marketplace where timing is often crucial. Managing precedents, helping their teams keep up to date in legislation, and providing responses to consultations are just some of the ways that PSLs add value to the business.

Aligned to the support that our PSLs provide, we have a network of internal experts who can advise and answer questions on our areas of expertise and approve our know-how documents. We've carried out a piece of work to map and publish the names of our key experts to help anyone in the firm find out who knows what. This means the knowledge in the heads of our experts is available when we need it, and we know whom to ask to find out more.

Part of the strategy will be to make sure BLM has the right competencies in place in terms of knowledge seeking and sharing, as well as information literacy; an important step I have put in place in several organizations as I have rolled out their KM strategy. BLM staff need to know when and how to "self-serve" to find information, both from internal sources and to research externally. People who are demonstrating the right behaviors need to be recognized. It is really motivating to individuals who are using the most relevant systems and sharing their knowledge with their colleagues across the firm to be recognized for this, particularly at appraisal time!

The role of technology and process

In terms of technology and process, I am developing a taxonomy: a list of subject headings to help us categorize and navigate our information and expertise. Alongside this, I have set up a new knowledge space to capture our key content, appropriately categorized to make it easy to browse and find information. When we build the taxonomy, it is important to consider content from the client point of view: what sector(s) they might be interested in, if this piece of know-how is relevant and interesting and we want to share it with them via a portal or extranet or via our newly created Policy Blog.

I work proactively alongside our lawyers and with the PSLs to curate and manage the new KM space on our intranet. This content, together with the knowledge we generate internally, is used directly and indirectly in our work with clients, feeding into our business development and marketing processes, contributing to our external marketing campaigns and our training events for clients, as well as internally to improve communications and support projects and knowledge sharing across practice groups.

Communications

Communicating our progress is really important, both with staff and with our external clients. It helps to keep everyone informed and maintain momentum with our projects. We have worked closely with our internal communications team to launch the KM team strategy internally. This included a video where I explained what KM means to BLM (KM@BLM) and introduced people to the concept of knowledge management – this is a new concept for many at BLM so we need to make sure that everyone is on board at every stage of the process.

As part of this initiative, we asked all staff to complete a KM survey. The survey results have helped me to benchmark our current position firm wide, to set targets, and to measure our early successes. The information will also be used by the PSLs as a starting point to audit existing information stores and collections across the business and, if suitable, bring these into our new know-how system or link to the information from the know-how system as appropriate.

Building on the feedback from the survey, we are holding four KM workshops with attendees at all stages of their careers, and from business areas across the firm, in different office locations. I think it is really important for me to be seen; I want people to know who I am, what I represent for BLM, and how they can help me. Alongside my wider team, I will introduce the concept of KM again – reaffirming what we have already communicated.

We will also use the sessions as learning exercises. I need to understand the way people use and share information currently to do their jobs, and what is important to them. This will help us to prioritize the ideas and projects we have identified in our KM mind map, and to find out how we can improve our information flows to help people do their jobs more effectively and efficiently. We cannot do everything at once and we need to work out the most common themes so we can work on these first. Events like this are really important to get under the skin of the firm and find out what is really important to people. It is also a great way to identify change agents who will help us to spread the message and to raise general awareness surrounding KM initiatives.

External information

The information services (IS) team, part of KM, offers first class research capabilities. BLM recently consolidated its London operations into a single flagship office. As part of this move, we reviewed hard copy library provision and drastically reduced the number of books in line with our changing needs as a firm. Now, we just have a small collection in the London office, reflecting the most immediate needs of staff, and we have moved to accessing most of our content online. A large number of staff are working flexibly and require remote access to the firm's resources. Now, they can access the online content wherever they are working; from any of our offices, from home, or from a client's office. Lawyers are being trained to self-serve wherever possible, and the IS team attend other team and know-how meetings to help their colleagues understand the range of information at their finger-tips, and how they can use it in their work, wherever and whenever they are working.

Knowledge that is not specific to the legal sector is growing in importance for law firms, such as intelligence about our competitors and key developments in our clients' businesses and the sectors in which they operate. Legal KM professionals are finding that they need to start looking at their own information and to access external information through this sector lens. In addition to increasing the number of subscriptions to online resources, we have recently been testing new tools to alert our lawyers to new developments in our clients' business sectors and industries, as well as to alert us to the material our competitors are publishing and competitor intelligence. Our lawyers need short, succinct summaries with the latest headlines, meaning they are better briefed on what is important to their clients when they meet them.

What I've learned from other sectors

My experience in KM spans the energy, pharmaceuticals, biotechnology, professional services, and not for profit sectors. I also spent six years as the head of knowledge management at The Law Society in the UK. KM challenges are common across all sectors. It is fair to say that the legal profession was at the forefront in the early days of KM, recognizing the value of knowledge and know-how systems. The essence of KM is learning from, and improving on, past experience and I think the legal sector could usefully benefit from monitoring other sectors, understanding their approaches, and finding out what works and what does not with regards to collaboration, innovation, and creating new knowledge. Looking at what other sectors have done in encouraging and recognizing positive behaviors such as collaboration and team-working, as well as developing better facilitation skills, will help to make law firms more commercial and efficient in the quickly changing environment we find ourselves in.

Innovative tools and practices can be helpful in engaging people, but there is no substitute for getting the foundations right in terms of good basic processes, governance, and tools for capturing and re-purposing our knowledge, and identifying who knows what. Law firms have appeared to be more reluctant to adopt social networking tools and techniques because they are often, naturally, risk averse because of the nature of their work. This is now beginning to change, however, and we are seeing the benefits these tools can bring if they are used wisely.

Another area we need to continue to work on is supporting our lawyers and other internal teams in managing increasing pressures from information overload. This needs to be in tandem with helping them to share what they know for the good of the firm, and for the benefit of our clients. My view is that, to support this, we need to link reward and recognition strategies to sharing knowledge and to team work, as well as rewarding people individually for their work. Allowing them time to manage information more efficiently means time saved looking for an important piece of information. And in today's world, anything that saves time has to be a good thing.

10 tips for developing a successful KM strategy

1. Mind mapping tools really help capture and manage the complexity.
2. Communications are vital, but make sure you have something to say!
3. Start with some practical wins.
4. Don't expect people to "get it" straightaway.
5. Consider metrics from the start – what will "good" look like?
6. A survey will help you baseline and prioritize efforts.
7. A senior, well-respected champion will open doors for you.
8. Network to learn what's working in other firms.
9. Don't just stick to your own sector – others also have lots of useful tips and ideas.
10. Your business support partners in the firm are great allies!

Case study 3:

Weaving KM into the strategic fabric of today's law firm – Five keys to success

By Jennifer P. Keller, president and chief operating officer at Baker, Donelson, Bearman, Caldwell & Berkowitz

Law firms in the 21st century look, feel, and run very differently from those of earlier times. While professionalism and ardent dedication to the advancement of client interests are still the primary purposes for which law firms exist, success requires a myriad of additional tools that were not even in the tool belts of decades past – things like legal project management, alternative fee arrangements, and knowledge management (KM), to name but a few. Law firms are at varying levels of adoption of these tools. A common question that arises is: "How do we actually make these things work and become a part of the strategy that our firm is advancing?" While the focus of this article is specifically on the integration of KM into a firm's strategic fabric, the keys to success in achieving that are quite applicable to attempts to weave any significant initiative into a firm's strategy.

I am not a chief knowledge management officer or an IT professional. I am the chief operating officer for a firm with 750 lawyers and public policy advisors in 19 offices across seven states in the south central United States and the District of Columbia. I have come to that position only recently, after working at the firm in various practitioner and management capacities for two decades. I was both a practicing labor and employment lawyer and a practice group chair at the time KM emerged within the legal field, and I have been in firm management at practice group, department, and board levels as KM has moved from a traditional content generation role to a total practice management/consultancy and product development role within my firm. It is also not without import that the firm has been on the *Forbes* list of "Best Places to Work" for six straight years – we place a genuine emphasis on culture as a key part of our strategic planning. It is through that lens that we have been successful in placing emphasis on KM throughout the firm, and in determining how to advance our strategic plan, in part at least, with the advancement of our KM function.

While there are certainly many elements that must come together to ensure the successful integration of an initiative or new way of doing things into firm strategy, there are five keys that have emerged as central to that success within the KM context.

Understand the psychology of the attorney of 2015

It is no mystery that the economic downturn of 2008 and beyond had a profound impact on the legal profession. It has also had a profound impact on the individual attorneys who work within the profession. Understanding, appreciating, and embracing the mindset of today's lawyers is an essential part of convincing them that KM can and should be a part of their practices. I summarize that mindset by a comparison to the more historical mindset. While, prior to 2008, law firms and lawyers *evolved* (meaning that they did change, but changed very slowly – almost imperceptibly at times), client demands for efficiency and better value now require *revolution*. Lawyers are required to adapt and change quickly. The rules seem to change regularly, and reticence is dangerous.

The nomenclature has changed, and value is the benchmark. Instead of work/life balance, lawyers now face the challenge of work/work/life balance. What does that mean? It means that we have added an additional layer to work – the layer that now requires attorneys to learn the business of law and to spend time honing not only their professional craft but the logistics of providing that craft more efficiently. We combine those challenges with a stressful external world where many attorneys are in the "sandwich generation", and the related challenges that come with working with three or four generations under one roof at a firm. And, finally, attorneys of today are bombarded with information 24/7, and "solutions" to every problem in the form of emails and the internet.

Why is this key to the integration of KM? Because of this psychology, attorneys crave some measure of simplicity, comfort, and help to satisfy increasing client demands. It is becoming more and more obvious to them that they cannot do it alone. This provides an opening for KM. However, what KM cannot do is force attorneys to embrace complicated tools and processes without adequate explanation of how they help – KM cannot force revolution, but must provide respite and the weapons to aid the revolution.

Another factor at play is the acknowledgement of today's attorneys and law firms that investment in research and development is necessary. Firms must spend time and money to develop tools and processes that work for their practices and clients, and KM is an area of necessary investment. However, with attorneys facing increasing pressure to bill hours and produce revenue, asking them to invest non-billable hours in the effort is tough. In our firm, we established a program to give attorneys working credit for time spent assisting the development of KM functions. The program, originally called "KM Dollars" and now called the "Venture Fund", encourages investment and allows the firm to budget for progress each year. Without some kind of effort to compensate for investment, it is unlikely to occur.

Have a seat at the table

To become integrated into firm strategy, KM (or any other similar firm initiative) must have a seat at the proverbial and literal tables. This means that KM must be represented by either direct KM professionals, such as the chief knowledge management officer, or a champion or proxy at firm meetings where strategy is discussed, created, adopted, and advanced. If direct KM representation is not possible for whatever reason, the champion should be knowledgeable about both the technical and operational aspects of KM, and they should also be aware of and sensitive to challenges that could be raised by other members of firm management.

In my firm, KM is routinely present at strategic planning meetings, board meetings where essential KM functions are discussed and progress is voted upon, and department and practice group meetings where overall firm strategy is distilled to the practitioner level. KM professionals are also asked to interface regularly with attorneys at their desks and in performing day-to-day tasks to see how tools are being used and what could make those attorneys' lives easier So, suffice it to say that KM "sits" at many tables and with many constituencies regularly. Without that constant, multi-level interface, it seems nearly impossible for KM to determine how it can build bridges to help the firm meet its goals. Further, as firm management and lawyers alike see and hear from KM, they understand how it can help them address client needs more efficiently, and buy-in grows.

Focus on client value

While client value is not a new concept, the level of focus upon it is still fairly new and firms are still trying to understand what "client value" really means. The tricky part is that value to one client is not the same as value to another. We typically say that client value encompasses four intertwined concepts: lower cost, higher predictability, better outcomes, and more transparency. But does lower cost mean lower legal spend per year, lower cost per matter, lower cost per hour, or lower cost per task or phase? Does higher predictability mean predictability of spend, predictability of outcome, or predictability of course of the matter? Does better outcome mean less cost, a pure "victory" (however that is defined), or the predictability mentioned already? Finally, does transparency mean a clear picture of costs as they are incurred, a full view of the matter's processing and work within a firm, or just an increased lawyer/client dialogue?

Client value is defined and determined by the client, and lawyers want to understand what it means to their clients. Once they know what their clients perceive as value, they then want to understand how they can provide that value without sacrificing quality of professional service. That is, of course, where KM can come in. If the KM professionals within a firm strive to understand what clients want and how lawyers are falling short, they can help bridge that gap. If lawyers understand that KM can help them provide value, and not just that KM is the "new way of doing things" or some "fancy new technology that we have spent a lot of money on", the dialogue changes and interest rises.

Not unlike many firms, our firm has a client survey program through which we seek to learn more about client satisfaction and preferences, and how our service has aligned with those. While it would be fairly simple to share that feedback only with directly involved attorneys, we share it with various administrative groups (including KM) who can benefit from hearing the lessons learned, and we share it with all of our attorneys fairly regularly. We have seen that the KM function routinely takes the lessons from those surveys and works to provide tools to our attorneys or products for our clients that meet expressed needs. When that happens, there is no doubt that KM is helping deliver value.

Do not forget the importance of support staff and other administrative departments

Even once something like KM receives a position of prominence within a firm's stated strategic planning, it has not really become woven into the strategic fabric until adoption and execution are a reality. While the role of the legal assistant has also morphed, not only since 2008 but radically over the last few decades, it is still true that assistants are integral to attorneys' practices and can be invaluable in attorney conversion to a new way of doing things.

Take, for instance, the transition of most firms to electronic timekeeping from old-fashioned timesheets. In many situations, legal assistants were critical to adoption – they trained the attorneys, encouraged use, and found and passed along shortcuts. Slowly but surely, the transition happened. While we may no longer have the luxury of moving slowly but surely, those assistants can play a key role in the adoption and use of KM, and making them champions of KM efforts will pay huge dividends.

Similarly, other administrative departments can play an important role in KM integration. If legal project management, firm libraries, timekeeping, costing, and marketing are all working in tandem with KM – and in fact are integrated by it – all functions are more likely to be used, and used correctly. Moreover, those working in these functions, as well as those working in human resources, billing, new matter intake, and other administrative departments with whom the attorneys regularly interface, can help inform the KM function. They know what information attorneys routinely ask for and how they need to use it.

Identify and help remove obstacles

To be an embraced part of strategy, it is important that leaders of any initiative both understand that mindset and also *proactively* seek to make things easier. That concept is at the very core of what KM seeks to do. However, it is also quite possible that the tools and processes developed by KM are useful and quite impressive but, for whatever reason, they are not used by attorneys as originally envisioned. That is usually because, rightly or wrongly, they are perceived as too complicated or a waste of time, or the attorney simply is not even aware of the tool or process. In other words, even when wonderful tools exist, there are often obstacles to their use. Those obstacles will be different in every firm and maybe even in every group within the firm, but they do exist and can work to make even the most impressive KM advancement moot

Another important concept to remember in this regard is that perception is reality. Even if a tool or process is deemed entirely perfect by KM, if users do not see it that way and thus do not use it, it is not perfect. If users see obstacles or problems, it is hard to talk them out of those. A fix or removal of the obstacle is typically required.

A final point with regard to tip number five is that communication is king. Communication is essential to determine what KM tools are needed and desired: it is needed when rolling out those tools to make sure attorneys both know about them and how to use them; and it is needed when addressing lack of use or the resolution of problems. What does communication mean? Does it mean a blast email – one size fits all – to all constituencies within the firm? It does not if integration into firm strategy and success is the goal. The average US business person sends/receives over 125 e-mails in a day, and many attorneys send/receive more than that. Many of those emails contain time-sensitive client communications and must be the attorney's priority. So, if the only mechanism used to convey an initiative's message is email, one can expect that the message may be lost in a sea of "more important" communications. To be effective, communication must also include personal meetings, calls and training that is made available by more than one means, and the regular delivery of information at practice group and department meetings. We have found that communication regarding KM by attorneys themselves to their own practice groups is one of the most effective means because it evidences buy-in by a similarly situated practitioner.

There will always be some level of resistance to change. However, because of the state of the legal industry and the pressures facing those working within it, KM is uniquely positioned to advance at a speed that perhaps we have not seen before. By understanding attorney psychology in 2015, asking for a seat at the table, focusing on client value, seeking assistance from other administrative departments and support personnel, and focusing on obstacle removal, a KM team can ensure that its initiatives move forward and become a part of the very strategic fabric of their firm.

A version of this article first appeared in Managing Partner *magazine in August 2015.*

Case study 4:

Harnessing social channels to spread content

By David Laud, chief executive at Samuel Phillips Law Firm

Samuel Phillips was founded in 1920 – unsurprisingly by Mr Samuel Phillips, solicitor – and has always had its base in the heart of the historic city of Newcastle upon Tyne. The practice has six partners and provides high quality legal services and support for clients in the following areas: employment; family; commercial property; residential property; dispute resolution; wills and probate; and personal injury. Accredited with the UK Law Society's quality marks Lexcel and CQS, the practice prides itself on offering access to expertise at rates that give value as well as peace of mind.

In recent years the firm has introduced a number of innovations with the aim of keeping the practice at the forefront of the market and establishing the brand at a time when the sector in the UK faces increased pressures, including the deregulation of legal services. This will introduce non-lawyer-owned companies into the sector and will persuade already established household brands to broaden their service offerings to include the law.

Samuel Phillips identified that clients were generally a step or two ahead of the average legal practice when it came to communication. Firms were slow to adopt fax, email, and now text messaging, seeing only the dangers and risks, which prevented early adoption and an opportunity to capitalize on the new communication medium.

In 2014 the firm decided to completely re-design its website. The old site had become rather cluttered and content was not that easy to find. The new site offered clients the opportunity to "meet the lawyers" in the practice and navigate easily to the service pages. The following year has seen the site evolve and develop a regular and rich source of content.

Social media and Samuel Phillips

Samuel Phillips has had a strong view on adopting a social media strategy and is continually looking to develop and improve its presence and impact on its various sites. The view is that clients have taken to social media on a large scale. Many use the sites as their main form of online communication. Avoiding such trends can leave businesses "out of touch" and allow competitors in.

It has not been an easy ride – time is a precious commodity and many lawyers working long hours can find it hard to spare the time to develop the networks required online to make their social media activity truly successful. Social media features on the monthly management agenda and updates on follower counts, updates, and interactions are discussed. The firm is learning all the time and one clear lesson is that the true benefits are to be found once you have built a strong, trusted, and well-targeted network. Having thousands of followers and sending hundreds of Tweets a day is not the answer.

It is very much a "work in progress" for the firm, but in looking around it appears that on a number of fronts the firm is ahead of the curve and continues to press forward. Critical to success is the need to have attorneys engaged in the process.

Below is an overview of the social media platforms we use, and how we use them:

- **Facebook** – In 2008 the first Facebook page launched providing access to partner profiles and video content. The page has 526 likes and these are almost all generated from individuals who live and work close to the office in the north east of England.
- **Twitter** – The firm has two accounts dedicated to services and one account for firm-wide announcements and interaction. Launched in 2009, the main practice account has 1,700 followers with the majority being carefully targeted local individuals and organizations. Tweets are intended to engage with individuals in the north of England and to provide links back to new content created on the main and partner websites. The individual accounts are building their own strong communities.
- **LinkedIn** – In 2009 the firm began to actively build a presence on LinkedIn and started with a company page. Now followed by 244 accounts and with 30 individual Samuel Philips accounts which are all growing connections with their respective target networks.
- **FourSquare** (Swarm) – In 2010 Samuel Phillips created its profile on FourSquare (now Swarm) and included tips for fellow users to access the firm for a coffee and free introductory chat to discuss wills. The head receptionist is the "mayor" of the firm – that is the

user who "checks in" most at the firm. We find that the offers and tips generate footfall to the firm.

- **Google+** – Like many professional service firms, Samuel Phillips opened an account as a trial with four lawyers looking at the new social media site.
- The firm has also launched Instagram and Pinterest accounts, and is currently experimenting with video streaming sites Periscope, Meerkat, and Blab.

And there's more....

In 2009 the firm launched its SMS text service – "text LAW to 82010". This has proven to be popular with clients and additional applications for the service are planned for later this year.

Smart phone applications are an increasingly popular way for individuals to access information. It can save time browsing on the net, and these days a phone is never far from your hand. Samuel Phillips recently became the first law firm in England to launch an iPhone application to support HR managers and directors with a handy essential fact app for employment law. The firm has been very happy with the launch of the app which has now been downloaded over 1,500 times.

Summary

The experience of Samuel Phillips demonstrates that regional firms can take a lead with marketing matters and while there is still a lot of work ahead in developing our social media presence the foundations are in place and solid. The next target for the firm is to measure growth through meaningful engagement and network support measured by metrics such as Klout. The current score of 48 is a good platform for a firm of our size; however, we would expect to see our score rise within the next 12 months to nearer 55.

A "little and often" approach to keeping in touch and ensuring the firm's brand remains prominent is the simple yet effective approach taken. Expecting hundreds of new instructions through Twitter or Facebook is an unrealistic expectation, but if unprompted awareness research of brand recognition is anything to go by, it is certainly doing no harm at all.